INTRODUCTION

to

College Theology
Through Sacred Scripture

INTRODUCTION

to

College Theology
Through Sacred Scripture

A Course Designed for College Students

Sister M. Rose Eileen, C.S.C.

University of Notre Dame Press, Notre Dame, Indiana

NIHIL OBSTAT:
Reverend Joseph Hoffman, C.S.C.
Censor librorum

IMPRIMATUR
Leo A. Pursley, D.D.
Bishop of Fort Wayne-South Bend

Second Printing
March 1965

Library of Congress Catalog Card Number: 63-22222

TABLE OF CONTENTS

PREFACE

The course entitled, *Introduction to College Theology Through Sacred Scripture,* is presented as the fruit of discussions by a committee invited by Reverend Robert S. Pelton, C.S.C., Head of the Department of Theology at the University of Notre Dame, to consider and participate in its preparation. The meetings were held there during the 1963 summer session.

The course is tentative in its present form. Revisions made as a result of suggestions received from colleges adapting it as a pilot program in the immediate future will be subsequently incorporated.

The members of the committee are: Reverend Robert S. Pelton, C.S.C., University of Notre Dame; Sister Maria Assunta, C.S.C., Saint Mary's College, Notre Dame, Indiana; Reverend Thomas J. Barrosse, C.S.C., Holy Cross College, Washington, D.C.; Reverend James M. Egan, O.P., Director of Saint Mary's School of Sacred Theology, Saint Mary's College; Reverend Joseph E. Fallon, O.P., Trinity College, Washington, D.C.; Sister M. Gertrude Anne, C.S.C., Saint Mary's School of Sacred Theology; Dr. Cathleen M. Going, Loyola University, Montreal; Reverend Philip L. Hanley, O.P., University of Notre Dame; Reverend Thomas R. Heath, O.P., Saint Mary's College; Reverend William J. Hegge, O.S.C., University of Notre Dame; Reverend Hilarion Kistner, O.F.M., St. Leonard College, Dayton, Ohio; Reverend Carroll Stuhlmueller, C.P., Passionist Seminary, Louisville, Kentucky; and Sister M. Rose Eileen, C.S.C., Dunbarton College of Holy Cross, chairman.

INTRODUCTION TO THEOLOGY
THROUGH SACRED SCRIPTURE

Objectives

The primary objectives of the course are to develop progressively an ever deeper understanding of the concepts of Divine Revelation as God's Word uttered to man, and of the sources of its communication to him, in order that the student may acquire ability to use intelligently the proper method of theology in his subsequent courses in pursuit of a mature understanding of the Mystery of Christ, as well as of the meaning of his personal Christian response of loving faith to God Who speaks, submission to the message He speaks, and worship of Him "in spirit and in truth," which should be elicited through an understanding of God's Revelation and its sources. Such a course, therefore, as an introduction to theology through Sacred Scripture is intrinsically ordered directly to the general aim of the total college theology curriculum, and seeks to lay solid foundations for it, while at the same time it aims to achieve the particular objectives of what traditionally has been presented as a course in fundamental theology as such.

To develop the student's familiarity with the fundamental concepts related to the sources of God's supernatural self-revelation to man, the course presents the transmission of a well-ordered body of truth, both natural and supernatural, through a carefully selected sequential study of the Sacred Scriptures, both Old Testament and New; through directed readings and explanations of various areas of the sacred text itself, in order that the student may come to know God's revelation of Himself as One and Triune, as Incarnate; man's relation to Him in covenantal love; the Church as People of God and Mystical Body of Christ; and the revelation of God's meaning of a personal response to His Word in a Christian life of faith, worship, and moral conduct.

The basic structure of the course selects for its emphases the areas of thought traditionally associated with fundamental theology, but organized in such a way that its concepts are presented in a biblical context for the most part, and psychologically, rather than abstractly through a logically developed pattern. In the structure and presentation of the course every effort has been made to incorporate recent authentic psychological principles of the teaching and learning process. There is no attempt to present Sacred Scripture "in totum," nor under the formality of scientific biblical exegesis, but rather through certain selected pertinent areas of the sacred text unified sequentially and conceptually, and ordered basically in a historical development of the revelation of the Mystery of Christ, but according to the specific finality of a course providing an introduction to theology. The emphases imposed by such an end have been of primary concern.

The commentary on the selections from Sacred Scripture introduces the student to the fruits of contemporary biblical and theological scholarship, in so far as these are related to the objectives of the course, namely, to an intelligent familiarity with the sources of Divine Revelation, and in keeping with the academic competence and psychological development of a college student enrolled in such a course. The insights of modern theological speculation relative to the nature of inspiration, tradition, magisterium, etc., in so far as they clarify and enrich understanding and demonstrate the action of human reason seeking understanding of supernatural revelation; the valid principles of biblical interpretation relative to the particular selected areas of the sacred text considered in the course; deeper insights into these principles as they have been enriched through contemporary research in oriental languages, literary forms, history, archeology and the other ancillary sciences, are presented so that in keeping with the capacity of the students on this level of academic achievement, there may be developed a respect for scholarship in the profane sciences, as well as in the sacred, necessary for valid interpretations of the sources of Divine Revelation and for mature understanding of God's Word spoken through Sacred Scripture, Tradition, and Magisterium.

The communication to the student of an understanding of the respective traditions as they have been designated by scholars relative to the Old Testament should deepen his insight into the importance, necessity, and meaning of oral communication and preservation of God's Word antecedent to the composition and subsequent canonicity of the Scriptures. Likewise, the various problems relative to the question of inspiration of compiler, editor, etc., should come alive through study of the sacred text as it is proposed in this introductory course. Such direct contact of the student with Sacred Scripture should develop incidentally, though not as a primary objective, a broad knowledge of the Divine Mysteries, and awaken an awareness of his need to penetrate each of them more deeply and formally in subsequent theology courses. Moreover, as it is structured, the course seeks to integrate a richer understanding of the liturgy, and with proper related assignments for personal reading, aims to bring a familiarity with another area of Christian living into which the student cannot be effectively introduced too early in his college life. In each and every area of the course as it develops, he should be introduced to and made responsible for thoughtful, intelligent reading of the best and most pertinent materials available today to the educated layman, but selected with reference to the particular unit of study under consideration, at any given period.

In the broad sense, then, the course presented as an introduction to theology through Sacred Scripture should formulate in the student's mind something of a synthesis for all his subsequent study of theology and a life rooted in theological truth. Ultimately, through gradual progressively deepened *understanding of the fundamental concepts* around which the course is structured, he should come to an intelligent awareness of the meaning and implications in his own life and in that of the Mystical Body of Christ of which he is a member, of the concept of God's Word as He uttered It through the human instruments to whom He communicated It and inspired Its writing in the Scriptures of the pre-Christian period of history; through the words and deeds of the Incarnate Word in His earthly life communicated through the oral traditions of the apostolic era of Christianity and through the inspired writing of that Word in the New Testament; and that same Word preserved, interpreted, communicated, and defined through the magisterium of the Mystical Body of Christ. The act of that living magisterium using the sources of Divine Revelation in interpreting and defining a point of doctrine in our own age can best be made intelligible for the student, perhaps, through a carefully directed study of the *Munificentissimus Deus.*

Only toward the end of the course as it is here outlined, during which the student will have been acquiring some training in logic, should an effort be made to transpose the thought patterns which have been developed throughout the course into the abstract formal theological definitions of revelation, inspiration, tradition, magisterium, etc., the basic concepts of which will have been presumably deepened in his understanding. The formal pattern of the course in fundamental theology as it has been traditionally taught might then emerge designedly as a logical framework of reference and review for the course as a whole.

Content of the course

Basically, the Old Testament selections have been unified around the development of the concept of Yahweh and of the promises of salvation, despite man's failure to respond in loyal fidelity to God speaking through His loving act of creation and elevation of man. The scriptural narrative of the divine election of the patriarchs in the formation of the People of God to whom He communicates His repeated promise of salvation; the election of Moses; the Exodus; the Sinaitic Covenant; the important progressive divine acts of intervention in the subsequent history of His people; the continuance of His promises through David and the Prophets, culminating in the proclamations of John the Baptist, form the substance of the Old Testament areas selected for study.

The transcendent fulfillment of Israel's hope in Christ is presented through pertinent selections from the Gospels to bring the student into Christ's revelation of the Trinity, the Church as the promise and fulfillment of His continual presence with the Israel of the New Law and Covenant in the communication of supernatural truth and life; the act of redemption seen integrally through the Passion, Death, Resurrection and Ascension of the Incarnate Word as perfect Mediator with the Father; the coming from the Father and the Son of the Holy Spirit to communicate through the Mystical Body of Christ a participation in the truth and life of the Trinity; the concept of the liturgy as worship of the Father through Christ and His subjective redemption of men through visible sacrifice and sacrament. The unifying concept throughout this section of the course is the revelation of the Mystery of Christ.

The background for an understanding of the Mystical Body of Christ under the concept of magisterium is presented through an ordered selection of scriptural texts from the Acts of the Apostles developed through the concept of the Holy Spirit acting through Peter and the Apostles in doctrinal and disciplinary decisions of the apostolic Church, with a further development of the concept of the Mystery of the Church from the epistles of St. Paul under the analogies of Body, Spouse, Corner-stone, Elder Brother, etc. The concept could be further unified and clarified for the purposes of the total course through a pertinent study of the encyclical, *Mystici Corporis*. It is presumed that the theology of the Church will be presented in a formal course subsequently.

In order that the student may be brought to an awareness of the action of the Church in interpreting and defining revealed truth and seeing its use of the sources of theology in such action, a summary study of the Apostolic Constitution, *Munificentissimus Deus,* has been found effective. The document is especially pertinent in the course since its content has been written in the life span of our present generation of collegians and demonstrates for them the prudent use of all the related ancillary profane sciences, as well as the sacred, in the effort of the Church to determine the existence of the doctrine of Our Lady's Assumption in the deposit of faith found in the sources of Divine Revelation. The study of this document could well be used as a summation of the basic principles of the course as a whole, but specifically related to a doctrine formally and infallibly *defined as revealed* only in the twentieth century.

Suggestions to the teacher

The course has been structured so that it may be adjusted accidentally to the particular student capacity, need, and interests. It is not expected that all the suggested readings and directives be included in the activity of any one student. The directives pinpoint emphases which the lectures, class discussions, and student learning activities should follow. The teacher is free and urged to select, modify, and increase such activities to fit his own teaching situation.

In order that the course may serve the objectives toward which it has been constructed it is essential that *each student have easy access* to the commentaries listed from the *Old Testament Pamphlet Bible Series* (Paulist Press) and the *New Testament Series* (Liturgical Press), which have been selected for the respective units of the course. The student must be trained to read these commentaries intelligently and purposefully; the role of the teacher is to give enrichment to their content through his own class presentations, and to motivate and direct the student's own learning activities related thereto. Unless this procedure is followed and the student develops competence in such reading and study, the course cannot hope to achieve the objectives to which it has been ordered.

First Unit - The Book of Genesis

Basic texts for the student

Ignatius Hunt, O.S.B. *The Book of Genesis,* Parts I and II. New York: Paulist Press, 1960.

Neil J. McEleney, C.S.P. *The Law Given Through Moses,* Introduction to the Pentateuch. New York: Paulist Press, 1960.

Supplementary readings for the student

Thomas Barrosse, C.S.C. *God Exists.* Notre Dame: University of Notre Dame Press, 1963.

Celestin Charlier. *The Christian Approach to the Bible.* Westminster, Md.: Newman, 1958.

Peter Ellis. *The Men and Message of the Old Testament.* Collegeville, Minn.: The Liturgical Press, 1962.

Ignatius Hunt, O.S.B. *Understanding the Bible.* New York: Sheed and Ward, 1962.

Alexander Jones. *Unless Some Man Show Me.* New York: Paulist Press, Deus Books, 1962.

——————. *God's Living Word.* New York: Sheed and Ward, 1961.

John McKenzie, S.J. *The Two-Edged Sword.* Milwaukee: Bruce, 1956.

Frederick L. Moriarty, S.J. *Introducing the Old Testament.* Milwaukee: Bruce, 1960.

9

E. Kraeling. *Bible Atlas.* Chicago: Rand McNally.
The Bible Today.
Westminster Bible Atlas.
Worship.

Suggested sources for the teacher

W. F. Albright. *Archeology of Palestine.* Baltimore: Penguin Books, 1960.

————. *From the Stone Age to Christianity* (Rev. ed.). New York: Doubleday, Anchor Books, 1957.

Bernhard W. Anderson. *Understanding the Old Testament.* Englewood Cliffs, N. J.: Prentice-Hall, 1957.

Jean Danielou. *The Bible and the Liturgy.* Notre Dame: University of Notre Dame Press, 1956.

————. *From Shadows to Reality.* London: Burns and Oates, 1960.

————. *Holy Pagans of the Old Testament.* Baltimore: Helicon Press, 1957.

Roland DeVaux. *Ancient Israel, Its Life and Institutions.* Translated by John McHugh. New York: McGraw-Hill, 1961.

George S. Glanzman and Joseph Fitzmeyer. *An Introductory Bibliography for the Study of Scripture.* Westminster, Md.: The Newman Press, 1961.

L. H. Grollenberg. *Atlas of the Bible.* Translated and edited by Joyce Reid and H. Rowley. New York: Thomas Nelson, 1956.

Charles Hauret. *Beginnings.* Dubuque: Priory Press (paper back), 1955.

Jean Levie. *The Bible, Word of God and Word of Men.* New York: P. J. Kenedy, 1962.

Sebastiano Pagano. *Chronological Table of the Books of the Old Testament.* Ottawa: University Seminary, 1959.

J. B. Pritchard, ed. *Ancient Near-Eastern Texts Relating to the Old Testament* (rev. ed.). Princeton: Princeton University Press, 1955.

A. Robert and A. Tricot. *Guide to the Bible,* Vol. I (rev. ed.). New York: Desclee, 1960.

Chapter 1, "Inspiration" by P. Benoit, pp. 8-65.

Chapter 5, "The Books" by Chaine, Huby, Gelin, and Robert, pp. 171-183 (Genesis).

Aldo J. Tos. *Approaches to the Bible: The Old Testament.* Englewood Cliffs, N. J.: Prentice-Hall, 1963.

Gerhard von Rad. *Genesis.* Philadelphia: Westminster Press, 1961.

G. Ernest Wright. *The Old Testament Against its Environment.* London: SCM Press Ltd., 1950.

————. *Biblical Archeology* (2nd ed.). Philadelphia: Westminster Press, 1957.

Cf. bibliographies and related articles in *Catholic Biblical Quarterly; Theology Digest; Scripture; Worship.*

Proceedings of the Society of Catholic College Teachers of Sacred Doctrine, 1955, 1956, 1957, 1958, 1959, 1960, 1961, 1962, 1963.

The Book of Genesis could be presented according to the following divisions for the purposes of class presentation, assigned readings and discussions:

1. Genesis 1 - 5
2. Genesis 6:1 - 11:26
3. Genesis 11:27 - 25:18

4. Genesis 25:19 - 36-43
5. Genesis 37 - 50

The more carefully and thoroughly this first unit of the course is developed for the student, the easier will be the progress which can be made in subsequent units. The principles must be established here.

Specific objectives

To introduce the student to an appreciation and understanding of the meaning of Divine Revelation and inspiration, by effecting through class explanations and student readings of the biblical text and its commentary, as well as through related suggested readings and assignments.

I. A familiarity with the Book of Genesis so as to deepen an understanding of:

A. God revealing Himself in the act of creation as that act is set forth in the creation account in the inspired text.

B. God revealing Himself in His acts of election of the patriarchs whom He selects and commissions to be the human instruments through whom he is to prepare a People of God who shall continue to communicate Divine Revelation to all men of all times and all places.

C. God's acts of intervention in salvation history of the patriarchal period; the history of man's failure to respond in loyal attachment to God acting for him and speaking to him, and God's constant pursuit, so to speak, of the loyal response of His creatures, despite their sin. Emphasis here should be placed on sin as the failure of personal response to God's message, rather than on the moral analysis of the species of each sin.

II. A familiarity with God's inspired Word in Genesis in order to develop in the student's mind an understanding of:

A. The place that oral tradition played in the history of the development of this book of the Bible which might be called the Preface to the Pentateuch. This concept should be clarified through the study of the specific traditions, Y, E, and P (Yahwist, Elohist, Priestly), which entered into its composition. It is a necessary basis for an understanding of the action of the inspired author in the collection, selection, and writing of these traditions under the action of God as principal author of Sacred Scripture.

B. Literary forms used by the inspired author in the communication of these traditions in which God's Revelation had been preserved and communicated before the existence of the Bible itself. The following literary forms found in Genesis should become familiar to the student as a result of his study of this first unit of the course:

1. The highly schematic pattern chosen for the six days of creation account in Genesis (cf. *A Path Through Genesis and Beginnings*).

2. The symbolism and imagery of the Garden, an oriental pattern of expression, to communicate the theology of the first sin of man, and the psychological analysis of the temptation and fall of Adam and Eve, rather than a strictly historical description of how the first sin was committed.

3. Ancient "scraps of genealogy" and sketchy documentation recalled from memory, used to carry along the theology of salvation history which is the purpose of the sacred writer.

4. The literary device of "inflated numbers" to cover the prehistoric period for which the sacred author has no library of historical sources for his information.

5. The oriental literary form which might be called the *saga*—a popular tradition which retained and emphasized significant facts, while rearranging, telescoping, or elaborating their accidental settings and circumstances to set forth in the clearest possible light the essential truth of the events, namely, God's salvific acts in history. (Story of Abraham, Isaac, Jacob.)

C. The differences between the modern concept of history as it has developed during the past century, and that of "mediated history" or "salvation history" as it is recorded in the Bible.

D. The scientific notions commonly accepted by the people of the ancient Near East at the time of the composition of Genesis, as opposed to the knowledge of the various sciences as they have developed during the past hundred years through study, research, and experimentation. For the sacred writer to have known the science of the twentieth century, God would have had to reveal data to him, which in God's Providence and governance of the universe, He had given His rational creature the natural powers to discover through long and patient efforts.

E. The gradual development of understanding of the covenant relation as it is found in Genesis; the notion of covenant as it has been enriched through recent archeological and historical studies and its implications in the covenants with Adam (his supernatural elevation to grace), Noe, Abraham, etc. The deepened understanding of the meaning of the covenantal relation with God initiated by Him in gratuitous election of His creature and the concommitant privilege and obligation of the creature's response in loyal fidelity to God's Word and act.

F. The gradual deepening of the student's understanding of the principle of "sign and symbol" which distinguished the respective covenants which God established with man: the rainbow with Noe; circumcision with Abraham; preparation for this principle as it will unfold subsequently in theology.

(1) Note the symbol of the serpent to give a derogatory touch to the image of "other gods."

G. The gradual deepening of the understanding of the activities of the sacred author of Genesis by which as a rational human instrument under divine inspiration he is the subject of the simultaneous human and divine activities necessary to write God's inspired Word; the close compenetration of the two causes which work in harmony to produce the single effect; emphasis on God's action of the human author freely moving his faculties so that he acts freely, but under the divine enlightenment and impulse patterned according to man's freedom.

H. Clear distinction through pertinent illustrations of data in Genesis between revelation and inspiration; between natural revelation and Divine Revelation, as opportunity may be presented through presentation of explanations of the text and through questions which may be proposed by students.

Throughout the study, it is assumed that the student will be made responsible to read carefully over a period of some three or four weeks, while the class lectures and discussions are deepening understanding of the more difficult areas, the commentary on the Book of Genesis, Parts I and II prepared by

Father Ignatius Hunt, O.S.B., and to be responsible to master the key sequential episodes around which the book is developed. Factual data, such as might be necessary for a satisfactory performance on the "Self Teaching Quiz" appearing at the end of each of the two pamphlets is to be the personal responsibility of each student. A brief factual test might be prepared periodically for the class, but should be kept to a minimum of time during the class period. Emphasis as far as the actual class period is concerned should be placed on the development of the understanding of the student of what is meant by "God revealing Himself" through His acts of creation and election of His creatures; an even deeper penetration of the meaning of those divine acts by His creatures who preserve and communicate that revelation orally in the prebiblical times; the explanation of the various written traditions which came to be made as the instruments for writing were developed; and the compilation and editing of those traditions in the characteristic literary forms, and historical and scientific modes of expression of the period of time in which the human author selected by God as His inspired author wrote.

In regard to the development of the idea of inspiration, the study of Genesis is designed to emphasize in the student's mind the reality of the human author as rational; his dependence upon natural activities in the selection, compilation, and writing of the data of the sacred text, limited by the environment and milieu in which he lived; yet under the divine action in communicating in writing what God willed that he should communicate, and that for men of all ages, cultures, and places in human history. The question of transmission of the text should also be introduced in this study of Genesis in pertinent sections, although in subsequent books treated, the question will appear more frequently. Every effort should be made to purge from the student's interpretation of the sacred text, the Fundamentalist approach which so frequently conditions students' attitudes toward the Bible.

The following suggested directives for the student's personal activity in attaining the objectives of the course are designed to give a broad familiarity and synthesis of some subjects treated in this unit, and to concentrate their efforts purposefully thereto.

1. The divine act of creation as it is narrated in Genesis is set in the pattern of the *history of God's acts of salvation* in the period of the prehistory of the human race used as a framework of reference for this first book of the Bible, probably written after the end of the Babylonian Exile in 538 B.C. There are other passages in Holy Scripture where meditation on this divine act of creation is used in a pattern suited to the prayer-life of God's chosen people. Read the description of creation and God's care for the universe in Job 38-41. Notice God is presented here as speaking Himself on the subject of creation. Indicate how this description should influence your attitude to God's world, if you are to think theologically about it. Read also the following Psalms: 148, 103, 8, 28, and Daniel 3:51-90, which are prayers inspired by God in which the creation theme is made the subject of loving praise of Him. Cf. Col. 1:15.

2. From your study of Genesis, select passages therein which illustrate the principle that God in revealing Himself acts and speaks through secondary causes; that in governing His creatures He also effects that governance through human agents. Show how this pattern is followed in the content of Genesis. What characteristics of Yahweh as a personal God and as a redeemer emerge as He is revealed in Genesis? Watch carefully as you continue your study of God's inspired Word in this course for further insights into the distinctive characteristics of the God of Israel.

3. As you have learned through your study of Genesis, the Semitic mentality in describing God's acts cuts through, so to speak, any reference to secondary causes and attributes the effect to God directly. How would such an attitude of mind in one seeing the tremendous achievements of men in the natural sciences place those men and their achievements in proper focus in relation to God in the thought of one who is familiar with His revelation? In such a view, how does science itself come to be seen as the act of God in, through, and for man? God acting through creatures in His governance of the universe will be developed in your subsequent theology courses. God gives His rational creature a share in the work of bringing the universe to the service of man in his life of loving fidelity to God: "till the earth and subdue it." Observe evidences of this reality as it appears in your further study of the Bible.

4. From your reading and study relative to Genesis, prepare an outline indicating specific instances which the profane sciences of archeology, oriental languages, etc., have in recent years contributed to a deeper and more accurate understanding of God's inspired Word in Sacred Scripture. This outline, you will find, can be greatly enriched through your subsequent study of this course. It might serve later as data for an interesting term paper in courses other than theology!

5. In your reading of the Missal, be careful to observe and seek to understand the many references there to Noe, the Ark, Abraham, circumcision, Isaac, Jacob, Joseph, Melchisedech, the "Covenant" or "testament," "light and darkness," etc. Read the liturgy for the Restored Easter Vigil and see its use of the creation theme. Read also the ceremony of Solemn Baptism. You should find that the course in *Introduction to Theology Through Sacred Scripture* gives you ever deeper insights into the beauty of the liturgy of the Holy Mother Church.

6. In your social contacts, you are likely to meet either a "convinced atheist" or one who assumes the attitudes of a pseudo-atheist, and likewise others who may either be pagans, or who live as if God does not exist. You will have found it profitable through the course to have an ordered developed insight into the distinctive characteristics of Yahweh as He is revealed in the Old Testament and those of the gods whom the pagans accepted and worshipped

among the peoples who were the neighbors of the Israelites in the ancient Near East. How does the modern pagan differ from the ancient pagans who had insight regarding a being greater than they? Read thoughtfully during the first part of this course, the excellent paper-back, *God Exists,* by Thomas Barrosse, C.S.C., University of Notre Dame Press. Other books will be recommended to you on the subject as the course progresses. They will prepare you to meet the attacks made in our contemporary world on belief in God and commitment to Him in a Christian life.

7. Study carefully the image of Abraham as a man of faith as he is presented in Genesis; analyze the various situations of his election and his role as father of the Israelites to see the response of faith in his life. What differences do you find in this study of the concept of faith, and the meaning of faith as you have understood it previous to this course?

8. Sacred Scripture is spoken of in the sacred text itself as a "two-edged sword." This description has been used as a title for a very informative book recommended for your reading. From your experience with this course, what would you say is the meaning of the expression?

9. How has your study of Genesis corrected and modified your previous ideas concerning divine inspiration?

10. Observe the response of the patriarchs to God revealing Himself through His acts of divine in-

tervention in their regard and see how that response is expressed in acts of worship identified as sacrifice. This idea will unfold and be enriched gradually through this course. A special summary or topical outline of these acts as you have met them in Genesis will be a help to you in developing a greater insight into their meaning and implications, through a similar effort followed with other books of the Bible which you will subsequently study and read in this course. The response of the creature in worship is a very important subject to watch throughout your course.

11. As you read either the commentary, the sacred text itself, and the assigned supplementary readings, list specific questions for which you wish an answer. Present these questions in written form to your professor who will answer them either in class, or through a personal chat with you, or he will indicate for you interesting sources where you may find the answers through reading.

Second Unit - The Book of Exodus

The Origin at Sinai of the Theocratic Unity of Israel

Basic text for the student

Roland E. Murphy, O. Carm. *The Book of Exodus,*
Parts I and II. New York: Paulist Press, 1960.

Supplementary readings for the student

J. Giblet. *The God of Israel, the God of Christianity.* Translated by Mother Kathryn Sullivan,
R.S.C.J. New York: Desclee, 1961, pp. 23-42.

Ignatius Hunt, O.S.B. *Understanding the Bible.*
New York: Sheed and Ward, 1962.

Alexander Jones. *Unless Some Man Show Me.*
New York: Paulist Press, Deus Books, 1962.

John McKenzie, S.J. *The Two-Edged Sword.* Milwaukee: Bruce, 1956.

Frederick L. Moriarty, S.J. *Introducing the Old
Testament.* Milwaukee: Bruce, 1960.

Mother Kathryn Sullivan, R.S.C.J. "The God of
Israel, God of Love," *The Bridge,* IV, 1961-1962.

Suggested sources for the teacher

Sections pertinent to this unit from bibliographies
under the first unit.

A. Gelin. *The Key Concepts of the Old Testament.*
New York: Paulist Press, Deus Books, 1962.

H. H. Rowley. *From Joseph to Joshua: Biblical Tradition in the Light of Archeology.* London: Oxford University Press, 1950.

Specific objectives

To develop familiarity with the Book of Exodus in order to continue to deepen the student's understanding of:

I. The history of the People of God as it unfolds through the acts of divine intervention in their behalf relative to the period of their deliverance from Egypt and their journey to Canaan.

    A. Moses' organization of the tribes as an amphictyony, i.e., tribes organized around a central shrine, the Tabernacle where God is actively in their midst with His presence and His power.

    B. The prophetic vocation; God's election and commission of individuals to be His spokesmen in the communication of His revelation; the emergence of the idea of the prophet.

    C. The idea of the first-born dedicated to divinity and the evolution of its meaning through the Paschal feast in Exodus 12.

II. God's self-revelation to His people.

    A. The gradual unfolding of the concept of monotheism through the words and acts of Yahweh (Exod. 3:14-15) and the implications of this revelation of His Name.

    B. The gradual unfolding of the idea of man's response to Yahweh and His acts of intervention in terms of worship, with the ideas of sacrifice concerning divine designation of the priest, and his attire in priestly acts, the place of sacrifice, the gift and manner of offering.

C. The introduction of the idea of liturgical feasts as they appear in the sacred text, Pasch and Azymes.

D. The introduction of the idea of the priestly character of God's people; they are His special possession who stand before Him in worship.

E. The development of the idea of covenant relationship culminating in the Covenant of Mount Sinai, the heart of Old Testament theology.

F. The introduction of the idea of Law expressed in the Decalogue and the Code of Alliance and how these differ from other ancient law codes.

G. The development of the revelation of the reality of God's presence with His people in:

    1. The Tabernacle ("God pitched His tent"), the place of covenant presence.

    2. Tent of Testimony, the place of God's presence in the Law.

    3. Ark of the Covenant.

    4. "Shekinah."

III. Traditions through a careful study of the inclusion, ordering and combining of the oral traditions of Y, E, and P in the text:

A. Introduction of the idea of the origin of these traditions in Israelite liturgy and familial celebrations; their preservation and communication through such channels before their use in the sacred text of the Bible; the continual preservation and celebration among the Israelites of their divine deliverance.

B. Note chain composed of links from various traditions to form an historical sequence: P in Exodus 1:1-5; Y in 1:6-14; E in 1:15-22; E in 2:1-10; Y in 2:11-22.

C. Exodus represents the crystallization of Israel's early spoken tradition concerning God's intervention in the history of God's people.

D. Development again of the idea that all traditions relating to Yahweh and His people are precious and important in content, even though some may differ in accidental details; characteristic of oriental mentality.

IV. Inspiration through an understanding of the use by the sacred author of the following literary forms which appear in Exodus:

A. The dramatic dialogue, "God said to Moses. . . ."

B. Dramatization and use of direct quotation (e.g., Exod. 1:9, 10, 15, 16).

C. Poetry of song in 15:1-18 (Song of Miriam). Cf. Song of Moses in Deuteronomy 32.

D. Cult epic in Exodus 1-15 read in a liturgical service of the Passover to commemorate the historical *act of God's intervention* in Israel's history and to glorify the God of Israel in a liturgical act.

E. The form of the suzerainty treaty as opposed to the parity pact common in the ancient Near East, adopted and adapted by the sacred writer to express Israel's unique relationship as a nation with the King of the universe; note the special characteristics of these treaties and the implications which follow regarding the understanding of the meaning of the People of God and their relation to Yahweh.

F. The storm and irregular phenomena of nature as a literary device to express God's presence and power.

G. The use of play on words to communicate ideas regarding the God of Israel and the relation of His people to Yahweh.

V. The contributions of the profane sciences of history, archeology, ancient languages, as they have enriched understanding of the meaning of the sacred text, as these are indicated in the commentary.

Suggested directives for students designed to give a broad familiarity with the subjects treated in this unit of the course and to concentrate efforts purposefully in regard to the general objectives of the course:

1. What further insights has the study of Exodus brought for a deeper understanding of oral tradition as to the part it has played in the forma-

tion of the text of Sacred Scripture? What deeper insights and greater clarification of the truths orally communicated by diverse traditions of the pre-Christian era is evident in the traditions as they are identified in Exodus? It would be profitable to take any one area of the text of Exodus where two or more traditions relative to the same event occur and make a careful analysis of the accidental differences in the diverse traditional accounts and see the value of recording these specific differences.

2. The prophetic call of Moses recorded in Exodus 3:1-4, 17; 6:2-7, 13 parallels in form that of three other major prophets in the Old Testament: Isaias, Jeremias and Ezechiel. (Read the following passages to analyze the similarities and the differences in the calls: Isa. 6; Jer. 1; Ezech. 1-2.)

3. God's revelation of Himself as Yahweh in Exodus 3:14-15 is the subject of much study and investigation among scripture scholars. You will find it interesting to read some of their conclusions regarding the meaning of this term. In your subsequent courses in dogmatic theology and in philosophy you will find that much of the philosophical analysis of the nature of God invokes the possible implications of this term. (Cf. Myles M. Bourke, "Yahweh, The Divine Name" in *The Bridge*, III, 271-287.)

4. Begin to make a topical outline of the development of the Israelites as a nation, as it begins to emerge in Exodus. This outline will be the be-

ginning of a more extensive one which will be developed in your study of the subsequent history of God's people. Observe, however, that whatever the pattern of their organization as a people and as a nation, God is working through human agents in guiding and forming them in their unique vocation.

5. In your study of Genesis your attention was called to the principle of the sign and symbol as manifested in the signs of the respective covenants with Noe and Abraham. Observe in Exodus again the signs of God's presence, the "cloud by day" and the "pillar of fire" by night, the radiance over the Ark of the Covenant indicating God's presence; the blood sprinkled on the door posts of the Israelites, the plagues, the crossing of the Red Sea, etc. Continue to observe evidences of the principle of sign. This subject will be important for your study of the New Testament relative to the sacraments in the Mystical Body of Christ, the new Israel of God.

6. Genesis, the wonderful account of cosmic, human and national beginnings, closes with an Exodus perspective in 50:24-25. Tradition looked back on this great event and idealized its theme which is that of glorious divine conquest. The theme of the Exodus has continued in liturgical cult of the Jewish people throughout the Old Testament and is still observed by them in the feasts of the Passover and Yom Kippur annually. Can you see how an intelligent understanding of this theme might be a subject

of dialogue fruitful in your contacts with Jews of our own day?

7. As you read your Missal, observe the many references to Pasch, Paschal Mystery, Exodus, "the dwelling of God with us" which you find in the text of the Mass. Continue to deepen your understanding of these references.

8. The People of God of each generation considered themselves personally involved in the Exodus through their yearly reminder that they went out of bondage with their ancestors. The liturgical recollection of Exodus was ordered to dispose the faithful Israelite to renew his covenant-love with Yahweh by which as a "people" they would again take Yahweh for their God and be His faithful people; He would be their God and they His dearest possession. Observe here the introduction of the idea of a corporate group, a corporate personality, which will be subsequently clarified and enriched in your future study of Sacred Scripture. As you study the New Testament you will come to see that the new Exodus, the complete Exodus of Christ through His death and glorification, is to be lived by Christians in the New Covenant through the liturgy and the sacraments. It will be important to keep in mind this subsequent meaning as you meet references to the Exodus in the later books of the Old Testament. It is an important theme in your present study.

9. From the revelation of Yahweh through His acts set forth in the inspired text of Exodus,

two dominant characteristics of the God of Israel emerge: that of His transcendence and that of His nearness to His people. Observe the contrast between Exodus 33:12-18 describing the "face to face" conversation between Yahweh and Moses, and Exodus 33:18-23 which serves to correct any mistaken interpretation of that nearness. You will find it profitable to read the following passages from other books of the Bible in which the same ideas are set forth: III Kings 19:11; Isaias 2:21-22; Job 28:9-10; Psalm 28:3-9.

10. The development of the idea of covenant as it is found in the Sinaitic Covenant recorded in Exodus introduces certain details which should be observed carefully for deeper insight into the meaning of the New Covenant when it will be subsequently studied. In the Sinaitic Covenant the inspired writer, acting under the influence of the principal Divine Author of the sacred texts, sets forth the covenant bond between Yahweh and His people under the common notion of relationship which the sharing of blood establishes, and through it makes a friendship pact with man; He gives to His people on this occasion a law to follow, a priesthood and a liturgy. To insure the holiness of His people, God pledges His abiding presence in Ark and Tabernacle. What clarification of one's own Christian life in relation to God do these ideas develop?

11. God's gratuitous love of His Israel and their failure of personal response in loving faith and

fidelity—such is the pattern around which the incidents in the desert are built. Study the incidents of Exodus 15:22 - 18:27 from this point of view.

12. The embodiment of the divine message in Sacred Scripture in human thought with all its imperfections, error excepted, has often been compared to the Incarnation of the Divine Word in human flesh, beset with weakness, sin excepted. This is a thought which should be fruitful for a student who seeks to come to deeper understanding of what is meant by the inspired text. Here in the Book of Exodus we have seen again the human words, the literary forms which, under the action of the Divine Author, the free human author has selected to bear the burden of the transcendent acts of God in behalf of His people of Israel. This and every other book of the Bible bears the marks of this double influence which produced it; it is at once divine and human—not divine with respect to the thoughts and human with respect to the words—but divine and human with respect to both. But the divine action will allow the limitations, and even the imperfections which are human to remain in the mind and in the language of the human author. Think about the reality "of the human self-abasement of the divine thought in Sacred Scripture," as it has been so beautifully stated by a great modern scholar, J. M. Voste. Can you recall sections in Genesis and Exodus which have deeper meaning for you in the light of this reality?

13. You will observe as you study the New Testament that it contains many passages which you can understand only in the light of what you have studied in Exodus. Recall St. Matthew's allusions to Jesus as the new Moses who leads His people through a new Exodus (Matt. 4 and 5); St. Paul makes reference to the incident in I Cor. 10:1-11; St. Peter spoke in terms of the Exodus when he instructed the early Christians, I Pet. 1:13-20; 2:1-10. From these few passages you will begin to see the truth of the statement: "One cannot understand the New Testament unless one knows the Old."

14. In your Missal read the following passages from the Easter Vigil service and see the use made there of the Exodus theme in the Second Lesson (Exod. 14:24-31; 15:1); the Third Lesson (Isa. 4:2-6); the Fourth Lesson (Deut. 31:22-30), and the great Easter Hymn, the *Exultet*.

15. Read the English translation of the words of the priest and the response of the people chanted at Benediction of the Blessed Sacrament and find the reference there to the Manna of Exodus. One can understand and interiorly participate intelligently in the liturgy of the Church only if one knows the Scriptures! Read an English translation of the Baptismal ceremony and see the use there of the Exodus theme; you will find the same theme running through the Masses of the Paschal season. Note also in the Baptismal ceremony the references to the creation theme.

16. Exodus gives the blueprint of the Kingdom of God; the People of God who form this kingdom are elected and elevated to the dignity of a theocratic nation, directed, ruled, and protected by Yahweh; the laws and regulations, the observance of which is to be their response to the acts of Yahweh in their covenant relation with Him; the form their worship of Him in loving praise and sacrifice is to follow; His abiding Presence in the midst of His people while He guides and protects them. You will find this pattern of the Kingdom of God which emerges in the Book of Exodus important in all your subsequent study of this course. Watch its features as you see them unfold.

17. Read the following Psalms to see the use that is made in them of the Exodus theme and the Sinaitic Covenant for the prayer life of the Israelite. These Psalms still form the prayer life of the priests and religious and many of the laity also in the Mystical Body of Christ today who pray the Divine Office of the Church. Remember, *these prayers are God's inspired words* and are therefore unique among all prayers privately composed: Psalms 113:1-8; 134 (you were advised to read this Psalm in connection with the creation theme; note now your deeper understanding of it in the light of Exodus); 135:10-22; 104; 105; 26-38; 78:43-50. As you come to know the text of Sacred Scripture, you will find by experience the principle which your professor will often indicate, namely, that the words have deeper meaning than even the

sacred author may have known them to have. They are the effects of divine and human action! You are gradually coming to penetrate their fuller meaning.

18. As understood by the patriarchs, in so far as He is revealed in Genesis, God is not local but protects them wherever they are; He has no traits of a god of nature, like those of their neighbors; He will not countenance any strange gods; He is kind with the kindness of a Father for His children, although the term "father" is not used of Him. In Exodus He is described as He "who brought Israel out of the land of Egypt" and identical with the God of creation and the God of the patriarchs; He is further revealed here as "He who is really and truly present" among His people and His existence is manifestly active. Can you add any other insights into the nature of God as He is presented in Exodus? Have you noticed the difference in the language of the sacred text regarding God from that which you have been taught in previous religious instruction? Do you know why?

Third Unit - The Book of Leviticus

The Organization of God's Priestly People of Israel around the Ark and Tabernacle

Basic text for the student
    Carroll Stuhlmueller, C.P. *The Book of Leviticus.* New York: McGraw Hill, 1961.

Supplementary readings for the student
    The same bibliographies as indicated for the first and second units of the course, according to the sections in each book pertinent to the unit.

Suggested sources for the teacher
    Jean Danielou, S.J. *The Bible and the Liturgy.* Notre Dame: University of Notre Dame Press, 1961.
    Roland DeVaux. *Ancient Israel, Its Life and Institutions.* New York: McGraw Hill, 1961 (sacrifice, pp. 415-417; feasts, pp. 468-517).

Specific objectives
    I. To develop general familiarity with the Book of Leviticus in order to show that in it is contained God's Word concerning the priestly character of His chosen people, the laws and rituals which are to be observed in their worship of Him, not only in ceremonial life, but in their

daily activities whatever they may be. "If you hearken to my voice and keep my covenant . . . you shall be to me a kingdom of priests, a holy nation" (Exod. 19:4-7). "You shall make and keep yourselves holy, because I am holy" (Lev. 11:44-45); "Be holy, because I, Yahweh, your God am holy" (Lev. 19:2, 20:7; 20:26; 22:31-33).

II. To develop the general idea of Israel's worship of Yahweh, emphasis should be placed on the following development of ideas:

   A. Sacrifice as to its essential elements.

      1. Divine designation of the minister; vocation or election and ordination.

      2. Divine designation of gifts to be offered.

      3. Divine designation of the manner of offering the gifts in sacrifice.

      4. Divine designation of the purpose or ends to which the act of sacrifice is directed.

      5. The distinctive meaning of bloody sacrifices as willingness to offer one's life (blood was regarded as principle of life by ancients), the best and most perfect gift, if God, the source of that life, should so will.

   B. Liturgical feasts of the Israelites as acts of corporate worship of the People of God, by which they participated in the acts of God's intervention in their salvation history and committed themselves to fidelity to the bond of covenant love.

      1. Yom Kippur (Atonement).

      2. Feast of Weeks (Pentecost).

      3. Feast of Harvest (Tabernacles).

      4. Sabbath Day, Sabbatical year, as well as the Year of the Jubilee.

      (Students should become aware of the importance of their understanding of these feasts in relation to liturgical feasts of God's people of the New Israel, and also from the point of view of the importance of such knowledge for intelligent dialogue with Jews in contemporary society).

C. Stress the *meaning* of the laws of the clean and unclean, etc. (not in details) but in order to develop understanding of the concept of ritual cleanness in general as the basis of holiness befitting *people consecrated to God*. This concept will be important for understanding later the formalism of the Pharisaical school and its repudiation by the prophets and by Christ.

III. To develop a clearer understanding of the Priestly tradition, for it appears in its fullness of purpose in Leviticus. Its characteristics can be most effectively discussed here.

IV. To continue to deepen the understanding of inspiration through clarification of what is meant by:

A. The attribution of this book to Mosaic authorship despite the evidence that it contains codifications of laws and customs of much later periods in Israel's history than that of the period of the life of Moses.

B. The use by the sacred author of ancient laws
and customs observed by pagan peoples of
of the Near East as a framework for the
laws and customs of the People of God
through which they are to respond in loving fidelity to Yahweh. Observe that the
ritual cleansings, etc., of Leviticus are
found in the history of many ancient religions and reflect customs indigenous to
the respective cultural patterns of the various historical periods of the ancient Near
East. Israel's unique contribution to these
customs, however, is that she gave a distinctive religious orientation to the various
elements of these cultural patterns. She
impregnated them with the spirit of the
Mosaic Covenant. Hence these laws were
said to be "spoken by God to Moses" and to
Aaron. Such expressions were the literary
device used by the sacred authors to stress
the fact that while many of the laws were
later than the time of Moses, they reflect
his spirit and are faithful to the traditions
of the Mosaic Covenant.

V. To give insight into the revelation of the whole
liturgical life of the Israel of God in the Old
Testament.

*Suggested directives for student's thought, reading
and study*

1. The author of the commentary writes: "These
laws (of Leviticus) bring everything in human
life under the control and sanction of religion;
norms of hygiene and medical practice, dietary

rules, and eating habits. These were not the days of distinctions and separations: church and state, sacred and secular, holy and profane. There would be something similar today if we were to 'sanctify' by religious obligation the practice of driving the automobile down the right side of the street . . . of wearing coats and hats on formal occasions." What meanings do you find in this statement relative to much that you hear and read today about secularism? What is secularism? The *spirit* of Leviticus, certainly not its details, should suggest the change in thinking we should try to effect in regard even to customs of daily life, if we are to begin to effect a change in the secularistic attitudes that are so common.

2. Notice in your reading of and about Leviticus that even the most *natural* customs and practices are thought in the mind of the sacred writer as somehow related to man's acknowledgement of dependence on Yahweh. Have you begun to see that your study of Sacred Scripture indicates ever more clearly that nothing in your life can be withdrawn from God as the ultimate source and cause, sin alone excepted, and even it is *permitted* by God! When you will have begun to realize that nature in all its aspects is God's gift, you are well on the way to begin thinking theologically!

3. How has your concept of the priesthood and of sacrifice been modified and enriched through your study of Leviticus?

4. In reading the commentary in relation to clean and unclean animals by Father Carroll Stuhlmueller, you must have been struck by another evidence of the data of the natural sciences throwing light on the meaning of God's Word. Did you ever expect to find that scripture scholars would need the help of zoologists and botanists in the work of interpreting sacred text?

5. Two precious fragments of the Book of Leviticus in archaic writing have been found among the Dead Sea Scrolls. Have you read about the discovery within your lifetime of these scrolls buried in caves for some two thousand years? Watch for references to them, even in the secular press. Can you see what would be the value of this discovery to the study of the transmission of the text of Sacred Scripture through the centuries? Would you be interested in reading more about this question of the Dead Sea Scrolls? Ask your professor to recommend a good list of easily available books and articles on the subject.

6. In your social and business contacts you may find it profitable by way of dialogue with Jews to know the meanings of their feasts and their relation to many that Catholics observe. All of them are rooted in Old Testament tradition. Your understanding of the Jewish liturgy will also give you deeper understanding of much in the Christian liturgy. Observe, as you progress with this course, data concerning these feasts: Purim (Book of Esther), Hannukka (I Machabees), etc.

7. From your study of the commentary on Leviticus and your reading of other references, explain what is meant by attributing this book to the authorship of Moses, when biblical scholars are quite well agreed that it did not reach its present form until the codification of the Priestly legislation which took place some seven centuries after the life of Moses? How did the act of divine inspiration effect that this subsequent compilation and editing of the text as we know it should have Moses as its author? Would God's action in relation to any other be necessary in preserving, communicating, and finally writing, the later codification? Explain.

Fourth Unit - The Book of Numbers

Israel's communal life in the desert organized around
God present in the Ark and Tabernacle

Basic text for the student

> Frederick L. Moriarty, S.J. *The Book of Numbers,*
> Parts I and II. New York: Paulist Press, 1960.

Supplementary readings for the student

> Sections pertinent to this unit from bibliographies
> under previous units.
>
> Louis Bouyer. *The Meaning of Sacred Scripture.*
> Notre Dame: University of Notre Dame Press,
> 1958. Cf. pp. 98-116 on Shekinah and its sig-
> nificance.
>
> Alexander Jones. *Unless Some Man Show Me.*
> New York: Paulist Press, Deus Books, 1962.

Suggested sources for the teacher

> Sections pertinent to this unit from bibliographies
> listed under previous units.

Specific objectives

> I. To present the salvation history of Israel in its
> transitional period between the liberation from
> Egyptian bondage and the formation of God's
> chosen people as a nation in Canaan, which
> under His guidance and protection, they will
> eventually conquer.

A. To deepen the student's understanding of, and appreciation for *salvation history* and the Hebraic concern for such history essentially because "it is a witness to the active intervention of Yahweh in their behalf"; to deepen the student's awareness that the Israelites came to know God and their relationship to Him in loyal fidelity of faith through this history which is to serve as a framework of reference, so to speak, for God's revelation of Himself to all men of all times and places.

B. The following are important for future understanding of the course and should be *discussed briefly:*

1. Israelites in the Desert of Sinai (1:1-10:10).

   a. Stress of the special. status of the Tribe of Levi.

      (1) The *priests* who are descendants of Aaron.

      (2) The *Levites* who are ministers of rank to assist the priests.

   b. Brief reference to the first annual celebration of the Passover in Chapter 9.

2. Journey from Sinai to the Plains of Moab (10:11-22:1).

   a. Moses and Aaron in punishment for their sin are not allowed by God to take the Promised Land (20:6-13).

(Note: Their sin is not to be interpreted as a sin of unbelief, but rather a failure to understand that Yahweh is merciful, and will provide for these difficult people because they are His people! Cf. Numbers 20:12: Because you did not trust me by *paying me due honor*.)

b. Aaron's death (20:22-29).

c. Eleazer succeeds Aaron.

3. On the Plains of Moab.

    a. Incident of Balac (22:2-24:25).

    b. Instructions concerning the conquest of Canaan (33:50-34:29).

        (1) Boundaries are defined (give only general plan).

        (2) Men who are to supervise the allotment of the land are appointed to serve under Eleazer and Josue. (Principle of division of authority and subordination in God's rule of His Chosen Israel!)

        (3) The forty-eight cities appointed for the residence of the Levites with pasture land; their means of support provided.

II. A. Through an analysis of the main incidents in Numbers to develop the student's understanding of Divine Providence; nearly all incidents have to do with the failure of God's people to obey and trust the leaders whom God has elected and commissioned for them — Moses, His Vicar — and the priests.

   B. To introduce through the analysis of the Balaam incident, the theological truth of the power of the Word of God; "for the ancient Semite the spoken word was more than a symbol; it had such dynamic power when uttered in proper circumstances and by the right person, that it accomplished what in reality it stated." This concept has immediate pertinence for the development of the concept of "prophet" as spokesman of God, the instrument of the Word, and remote relevance for the power of the Word in the theology of the sacraments which will later evolve in the study of the New Testament. This subject will likewise introduce the student to the beginning of an understanding of the distinctions between biblical inspiration and prophetic inspiration.

   C. To introduce the student through the Josue account in this text, to the concept of charismatic leaders—those men who receive from God, apart from any particular merits of their own, an outpouring of a divine gift or charisma for the benefit of others, to make up for human weakness; this may be related too in the student's thought, as another manifestation of God's providence in endowing certain men with eminent qualities of leadership in effecting God's acts of intervention for His chosen people. For understanding the progressive account of the Israelites, and God's governance of them through men, it should be made clear in the student's mind that Josue never had the full authority which God had given Moses, nor did he possess the same peculiar intimacy with God that was manifest in the case of Moses. Note that Josue was called "the servant of the Lord," as Moses was designated. Cf. Josue 1:1; 24-29.

III. In regard to deepening understanding of inspiration the following points should be emphasized:

   A. In the Balac incident, folklore is chosen as the literary form to carry the symbol of a profound theological truth which the sacred writer is communicating: namely, that God's Word "is powerful enough to make itself heard even through the mouth of a poor beast of burden." Interpretation of Sacred Scripture demands that we look to the intention of the author and distinguish the form he uses for the communication of his message, if the message is to be understood.

   B. Many of the literary forms and devices which the student has met in Genesis and

Exodus are again evident in Numbers. The student should show a more ready recognition of them and be able to identify them more easily, as he progresses through the Pentateuch.

Suggested directives for student's thought, reading and study

1. What evidences have you found in Numbers in regard to its commentary and your other readings relative to the book, of a more accurate interpretation of certain passages, through light received from the profane sciences of history, archeology, or philology?

2. Examine carefully Father Moriarty's commentary relative to Moses' sin in Numbers 20:7-13. Can you see here any principle which will be valuable for you relative to the proper interpretation of passages in Sacred Scripture? What principle, other than that of the competence of the commentator, is cited as necessary for the proper interpretation of this passage?

3. The principle of typology will be encountered often as you study Sacred Scripture. The Brazen Serpent incident in Numbers is cited in John 3:14-16 where Christ Himself alludes to this incident as a prefigurement of His own death. What insight into the meaning of typology does this reference give you?

4. Observe in Numbers 9 the Israelites' participation in the great act of the Exodus through the liturgy of the Passover they celebrated on

the first anniversary of their deliverance from Egypt. The liturgy is a *memorial* of the historic event. Note the presence of Yahweh here through the sign of the cloud and fire. He is present with His people in the liturgical act.

5. A careful study of the commentary relative to the two revolts against Moses, the one by Core against the religious authority of Moses and Aaron, and the lay rebellion of Dathan and Abiram, will recall to your memory the importance of careful critical analysis of texts which has been previously emphasized. This section, however, has more important implications in the theology communicated in Numbers; namely, the principle of authority. Later when you study divine governance of the universe in your dogmatic theology course, you will analyze the principle formally. God's revelation in Sacred Scripture, however, shows the importance of acceptance of the principle that all authority is from God and that through His creatures He governs men and nations.

6. "Tassels for remembrance!" What does this phrase suggest from your reading of Numbers?

7. Observe again in Numbers, the literary device of "inflated numbers," and that of "scraps of genealogy." Names of geographical locations which archeology has not yet been able to confirm, possibly the result of confusion which inevitably follows oral communication of data, are evident in Numbers. But again these discrepancies and lacunae are only accidental to

the purpose of the sacred author writing the inspired text, namely, to give an account of the active presence of Yahweh in the life, events, successes, and failures of His elect people on their way to the Promised Land of Canaan. Later archeological research may confirm biblical data or it may not. This is not essential for biblical interpretation!

8. Observe again the sacramental principle as it appears in Numbers. At this point in your study, you will find it interesting to compare the account of the sign of God's active presence with His people as it appears in Numbers 9, with the respective traditions with which you are becoming more familiar. It is described as a "column or pillar of fire" in Exodus 12:21-22 (Y trad); as "heavy cloud" in Exodus 19:16 (E trad); and the "glory of the Lord" in Exodus 24:16-18 (P trad). "Shekinah" is the general term which you will often find used in commentaries to indicate the sign of God's presence as such, although the word is not found in the biblical text.

9. You have found the Balac incident, Numbers 22-24, amusing and fascinating, certainly. Be prepared to discuss the significance of the following statements relative to this incident:

a. "Even decisions of pagan diviners are under the control of Yahweh."

b. "Yahweh can use any form of nature as bearer of His all powerful word."

c. "The zoology of the Balac incident is fantastic; the theology is very sound!"

d. "The arbiter of destiny is not simply the word of the prophet, especially a word uttered in complete independence of God. It is the will of Yahweh which decides the fate of men and nations, and the prophet is but the instrument of that word."

e. ". . . the spirit of God came upon him, and he (Balaam) gave voice to his oracle." (Num. 24:3). "To be seized by this spirit was the authentic sign of a divine vocation and God's assurance that He would be with him who spoke and acted in His name." Explain these words in relation to Balaam the pagan diviner.

f. You will recall that the patriarch Joseph in Genesis is described in the sacred text as having been favored with dreams which he interpreted in terms of future events. Balaam seems to have been the recipient of similar nocturnal experiences. Biblical scholars and theologians, however, are more inclined to interpret the literal words of the sacred text as meaning "intuitions." The principle which they follow in this interpretation is that God is author and cause of the natural, as well as of the miraculous, and that in ordering the events of history He does not multiply miracles. What is your reaction to this explanation? Does it tend to strengthen your response to God in faith or to question and delay that response?

10. Examine the text of Numbers to see the incidents there in which Moses acted as mediator with Yahweh for the people. This is an important concept to watch in your study of Sacred Scripture.

11. Read carefully the prayer of Moses in 14:13-19. Notice that in this prayer he appeals to all that God has revealed at Sinai (Exod. 34:6-7). Perhaps this may give you a hint as to the use you may make in your prayer-life of the text of Sacred Scripture in making known to God in prayer your thoughts and desires. What do you think?

Fifth Unit - The Book of Deuteronomy

Recapitulation of the Pentateuch in Discourses by Moses

Basic texts for the student
> George S. Glanzman, S.J. *The Book of Deuteronomy*, Parts I and II. New York: Paulist Press, 1960.
> Review Neil J. McEleney, C.S.P., *The Law Given Through Moses*, indicated for the first unit.

Supplementary readings for the student
> Same as indicated in previous units.

Suggested sources for the teacher
> Gerhard von Rad. *Studies in Deuteronomy*. London: SCM Press, 1953.

Specific objectives
   I. To introduce the student briefly to the Deuteronomic tradition, without at this time entering into the complexities of its formation and transmission any more in detail than that which is given in the commentary.
   II. The essential emphasis in the study of Deuteronomy is to be placed on the spirit of the priestly nation of Israel: the consciousness of God's love and His Will that Israel respond in loyal fidelity to Him.

III. The following outline will serve to unify the contents of the book so as to avoid emphasis on minor details.

    A. The First Discourse of Moses, 1:1-4:43.

    B. The Second Discourse of Moses, 4:44-26:19 and Chapter 28 (note the Law Code, Chapters 12-26).

    C. The Third Discourse of Moses, 29-30.

    D. Appendices, 31-34.

        1. Moses confirms the appointment of Josue, 31:1-8, 14-15, 23.

        2. The Law is left in care of the priests and the Elders, 31:9-13, 24-27.

        3. The Song of Moses sets forth the future unfaithfulness of the people, 32.

        4. Death and burial of Moses which serve as an introduction to the Book of Josue, 34:1-12.

Suggested directives for student's thought, reading and study

1. Note carefully the stylistic characteristics of Deuteronomy as the commentary discusses them; note also its characteristic vocabulary. Such observations should deepen your understanding of the fact that God's action in inspiration of the human author, does not modify the mode of speech or writing which is his by virtue of his education or lack of it.

2. In discussing the origin and purpose of Deuteronomy, the author of the commentary states his own position of thought relative to the compilation of the various sections of the book and his disagreement with the positions taken by other commentators. What light does this throw on the question of the freedom of biblical scholars in their efforts to obtain objective truth relative to various questions concerning the interpretation of the sacred text?

3. Select from your reading of the text of Deuteronomy, incidents reported which indicate the people's lack of confidence in Yahweh, and their consequent punishment by Him. What implications for our Christian life today follow from this fact?

4. The recurring theme of Deuteronomy is God's protecting love for Israel. Select the passages which you think most perfectly illustrate this theme.

5. Read Deuteronomy 7:6-8. How could you apply its meaning to your own election by God to the grace of Baptism and incorporation in Christ?

6. The believing Jew to the present time, has customarily recited three times each day a prayer which is called the *Shema*. It has been called the "Watchword of Israel." (You will find it in Deut. 6:4. Read this prayer in the light of the teachings found in Deut. 10:12-22; 11:13-21; and Num. 15:37-41.) What essential truths of Israel's religion are implicit in this prayer? Do

you recall that Christ recited the *Shema* in His answer to the question, "Master, which is the greatest commandment of the Law?" (Matt. 22:36). Note that He completed His answer with the commandment of love of one's neighbor.

7. Look up in a biblical encyclopedia the meaning of *phylacteries* and *mezuzah.* Do you recall in a previous unit, "Tassels for remembrance?" These were all interesting reminders for the Jews of the active presence and love of Yahweh. You will find Christ referring to them when you study the New Testament.

8. Biblical scholars regard Deuteronomy 6:20-25 and 26:1-19 as passages which are thought to be professions of faith that were recited during liturgical ceremonies at the Tabernacle which housed the Ark of the Covenant. Compare them with the act of faith which you have learned, and with the Credo of the Mass. You will observe that in the formula in Deuteronomy abstract or theoretical thoughts are absent. The expression of faith is rather a personal response of loyal fidelity to Yahweh for the "wonderful things of the Lord," that which you will often see referred to as the "mirabilia Dei," the wonderful acts of intervention in behalf of His people. This act of faith required of them a response of total commitment in loyal obedience to His Will expressed in the Law. What light does this give to your deeper understanding of faith in our Christian life?

9. Notice in Deuteronomy, Chapter 12, the important command concerning the destruction of all pagan places, in the expressions, "the high places," "sacred pillars" and similar ones. Similar expressions and commands will be found in other parts of the Old Testament. They refer to practices of worship of the pagan Canaanite fertility gods, Baal and Astarte, who, the people believed, were connected either with particular localities, or were cosmic deities. Their worship involved sacred prostitution in honor of the gods of fertility; hence the prohibitions against "high places" for God's people.

10. You will be surprised when you read Deuteronomy 2:34-35; 3:4-7; 20:10-18. This "herem" or ban practiced by the Israelites was a common custom among the ancient Semites. Read J. Levie, *The Bible, Word of God, and Word of Men,* pp. 240-245, on this subject. It will again bring you deeper realization of the reality you have wondered about previously in this course, namely, that God chooses men to achieve His purpose and He accepts their imperfections. Gradually He will lead them to the revelation of His Son to bring them to a higher concept of the law of love. But He only gradually educates these men through whom in human history He will act.

11. Emphasis on God's love of His people and His Will that they respond to that love in loyal fidelity to Him and His Will may be said to be the theme of Deuteronomy. Observe carefully

the following passages in the sacred text: 1:31; 4:32-40; 6:4-9; 7:7-13; 10:12-15; 11:1, 13, 22; 13:2-4; 30:6, 16, 20; and 32:1-20. You may find it interesting to compare the emphasis on divine love here with its expression in Christ's discourse at the Last Supper in John 13-17.

12. You could find a profitable review in Deuteronomy of so much that you have read and studied in the previous books of the Pentateuch. Would you be prepared to justify that statement?

13. For a further insight into the doctrine of love found in Deuteronomy you may find reading the following Psalms enlightening: Psalms 94, 80, 135, 99, 102 (a song of praise of God's love!), 104 and 110.

14. Chapter 34 records the death of Moses. The authorship of the Pentateuch is ascribed to Moses, and the decisions of the Biblical Commission would seem to confirm the point. How did he write the account of his own death? Can you explain adequately? What is the Biblical Commission and what are its functions?

15. In connection with your study of the Dead Sea Scrolls, you may be interested to know that a fragment of the Song of Moses from Deuteronomy 15 was discovered there. What importance would you attach to such a discovery in the light of what you have learned in this course?

16. The legislative code in Deuteronomy 12:2 to 26:15 is considered to be the heart of Deuteronomy and has named both the book and the tradition. Why is this true?

Sixth Unit - The Book of Josue

"God was fighting for His people."

Basic text for the student

Joseph J. DeVault, S.J. *The Book of Josue.* New York: Paulist Press, 1960.

Supplementary readings for the student

Bernhard W. Anderson. *Understanding the Old Testament.* Englewood Cliffs, N.J.: Prentice-Hall, 1957.

Celestine Charlier. *The Christian Approach to the Bible.* Westminster, Md.: The Newman Press, 1962.

Ignatius Hunt, O.S.B. *Understanding the Bible.* New York: Sheed and Ward, 1962.

Alexander Jones. *Unless Some Man Show Me.* New York: Paulist Press, Deus Books, 1962.

——————. *God's Living Word.* New York: Sheed and Ward, 1961.

John McKenzie, S.J. *The Two-Edged Sword.* Milwaukee: Bruce, 1956.

Frederick L. Moriarty, S.J. *Introducing the Old Testament.* Milwaukee: Bruce, 1960.

Suggested sources for the teacher

A. Robert and A. Tricot. *Guide to the Bible,* Vol.

I (rev. ed.). New York: Desclee, 1960, pp. 282-286.

H. H. Rowley, ed. *From Joseph to Joshua: Biblical Traditions in the Light of Archeology.* London: Oxford University Press, 1950.

Specific objectives

I. To acquaint the student with the theologically interpreted history of the Israelites during the period of their conquest of Canaan (1250-1225 B.C.), and the subsequent partition of the territory into Israel, the Promised Land.

II. To continue to deepen the student's understanding of the inspired author's use of literary forms for the communication of the Word of God. (Since in the Hebrew Bible, Josue, Judges, Samuel and Kings are classified in the collection of Old Testament Books known as the Former Prophets, and since the literary style and forms of these books have so many common characteristics, it seems advisable to follow this classification which is recommended by modern biblical scholars. The fact that they are classified with the historical books in the Christian tradition, can be easily explained to students. Stress the meaning of the prophet: one who speaks in the name of God; the prophet speaks God's word regarding past, present, or future. He preaches the faith!) According to the classification, as belonging to the Former Prophets, the following literary forms in Josue should be identified:

A. Josue is epic history, or "meditated history"; emphasis here should be placed on the two levels to be distinguished: (1) the actual historical event, and (2) the memory and use of the event for the author's purpose. Such "meditated history" is characterized by:

1. Hyperbolic exaggerations
2. Numerical exaggerations

} the "big picture" aspect.

3. The device of suppressing human factors involved in the reported incident.

4. Schematic use of sources in the compilation which results.

B. The form of the typical suzerainty treaty to record the covenant renewal in Chapter 24.

III. To continue to deepen understanding of the distinctions between profane history as such, and salvation, or meditated, theologically interpreted history. The content recorded in Josue is especially significant in terms of this objective. The book belongs to the Deuteronomic tradition. Its purpose is primarily didactic rather than historical and has been written to demonstrate God's fidelity in fulfilling His covenant promise to the Patriarch (Gen. 15:18 ff) and to the nation of Israel (Exod. 3:17; 23:23-33), i.e., that He would give them Palestine as their homeland. Other evidences of the author's didactic purpose are found in his insistence on obedience to God's command, for where the armies of Israel fail, it is because of Israel's disobedience (Jos. 6:18 ff; 19:14 ff), and emphasis on the fact that the conquest is the work of Yahweh, certified by the "miraculous" interventions by which His faithful people overcome the Canaanites.

IV. To present to the student a unified view of the contents of the book through the organization of its essential data around to following schema:

    A. The conquest of Canaan, Chapters 1-12.

    B. The division of the conquered territory among the "Twelve Tribes," Chapters 13-21.

    C. The return of the Transjordan tribes; Josue's farewell address and death; death of Eleazer.

V. To continue to deepen the student's awareness of God's acts of intervention in behalf of His people through secondary causes. The recorded incidents in Josue are especially significant. God's use of natural phenomena to achieve the victories of His people should be deepened through the careful study of scholarly efforts to interpret, without invoking the substantially miraculous, the following incidents among several others:

    the crossing of the Jordan, Josue 3:1-5:12;
    the fall of Jericho, 5:13-7:1;
    the failure and success at Hai, 7:2-8:29;
    the sun episode, 10:12-15.

VI. To develop and deepen understanding of the following concepts important for subsequent biblical and theological study:

    A. The solidarity of Israel as the family of Yahweh, through the study of (1) Achan's violation of the ban; and (2) the altar beside the Jordan, Josue 22.

    B. Faith
       Note Rahab; compare with Abraham.

    C. God's choice of the "weak things of the world" (Rahab!).

    D. Necessity of consulting the will of Yahweh before action: the Gabaonite incident, Josue 9:1-10, 27.

VII. Josue, if presented to students vitally, offers many insights into the place of *oral and written traditions* and the use of such sources for the written communication of God's word:

    A. Deuteronomic history introduced in this book which will combine Y, E, and P traditions for a new point of view.

    B. The use of profane documents for various geographical and historical details and customs.

    C. The use of Benjaminite Galgal (southern) cycle of stories of the conquest included in the final editing of Josue.

    D. The use of the Silo (northern) cycle of stories of the conquest.

E. The combination of sources for the two conclusions to Josue 23:1-24:33.

F. The interesting question of the silence of Josue regarding central Canaan—Samaria.

VIII. To give the student familiarity with the general geographical features of Palestine. Maps without too much detail should be used while teaching Josue, so that the location of the leading tribes, the major cities, the places of worship should gradually become familiar. Such data will form a background for the subsequent division of Israel into the Northern and Southern Kingdoms, etc.

Suggested directives for student's thought, reading and study

1. You have met Josue previously in your study of the Pentateuch. Review the background for his appearance in Josue (Exod. 17:8-14, 24:13, 32:17; Num. 13:16 ff, 27:18; Deut. 32:23). Be prepared to describe adequately the characteristics of this hero as he is presented in the biblical texts.

2. Many readers of Josue are annoyed by what seems to be its inordinate emphasis on geographical details. You may come to see the real significance of this feature, if you will keep in mind as you read that the Israelites had waited a long time for the acquisition of the land which was to be their own. They had not been landowners, but migrants, so to speak. The land which is now God's gift to them, the

Chosen Land, is very dear to His chosen people. It is to become the Holy Land!

3. Some scholars identify the theme of Josue in the words: "Yahweh was fighting for His people." Justify this statement and indicate its important theological implications which your reading of the text and commentary have clarified.

4. Rahab is an interesting biblical character. However serious her sins may have been she gains eternal renown because of her faith (cf. Heb. 11:31), and her good deed (James 2:25). She becomes too, one of the progenitors of the Messiah (cf. Ruth 4:18-22; Matt. 1:15). What is the reason, do you think, that the sacred writer was inspired to introduce her story in Josue?

5. The author of the commentary quotes the great biblical scholar, Pere Lagrange, as having said that "no book of the Bible bears such patent marks of compilation as does Josue." What did he mean? Illustrate the truth of the statement by a careful analysis of the sources for its composition which are treated in the commentary and other books or articles which you are reading concerning Josue.

6. The careful reader of Josue will observe passages, the sense of which is *contrary* to the "big picture" so characteristic of the epic. One such passage is Josue 13:1-7. Can you find other such passages in the text?

7. In attempting an explanation of the incident of Israel's forces crossing the Jordan in 3:1-5:12,

biblical scholars in recent years have sought every evidence to see, in the light of natural science, if it could be attributed to natural causes, rather than to a substantial miracle. From your readings, what are the explanations which you have found advanced from the natural sciences?

8. "The archeological discoveries or lack of them at Old Testament Jericho and Hai do not contradict the historicity of the victories which had to be won before the invasion of the highlands could be begun." Explain the meaning of this statement.

9. Note the paragraph at the bottom of page 13 of the commentary. This is the first time your attention has been directed to the necessity of knowing something of the various translations of the original Hebrew Bible and of its later versions. Consult a biblical encyclopedia for further information concerning the Greek Septuagint and other Greek and Oriental versions of the Old Testament.

10. Throughout Josue there are repeated instances of the author's evident disregard for recording secondary causes and human agents involved in the events. From a careful reading of the text, make a list of several such instances in which this characteristic is evident in the inspired text.

11. From your study of Josue, what changes have you experienced in your reactions to the rather common custom of designating unusual occurrences as "miraculous"? Are you beginning to

be more aware of the reality that God is acting for you continually through the laws of nature, other human beings, and through the whole reality of the signs of the Sacraments?

12. Father Ignatius Hunt, O.S.B., the author of the commentary you studied with Genesis, has stated relative to Josue that he had at one time listed in his class notes concerning the famous "sun stoppage" (cf. Jos. 10:7-15) some twenty different explanations of the event advanced by scholars. What are some of these explanations which you have come upon in your reading? What is the more probable and more commonly accepted explanation of the incident in contemporary biblical study? Can you see from this study the importance of analyzing the literary forms found in the sacred text in order to determine the intention of the sacred author and thereby the real meaning of the passage?

13. What essential principle is necessary for the correct evaluation of several questionable moral acts recorded in Josue, e.g., "herem"?

14. You will find it helpful as you read the Old Testament, to list the important places where stones are used to mark a spot in commemoration of an event, and where altars are set up! If you have not yet done so, begin with your reading of Josue.

15. You can add appreciably to your understanding of the assistance which related profane sciences give to biblical scholarship with your

study of Josue. Select instances where each of the following sciences are indicated in this role in the commentary (1) history; (2) archeology; (3) language; (4) natural science.

16. The theme of the crossing of the Jordan by Josue is linked in the writings of the Fathers of the Church with the crossing of the Red Sea by Moses as a symbol of Baptism. Why? Examine the text of the ceremony of Solemn Baptism to see if you find any evidence for this symbolism?

Seventh Unit - The Book of Judges

Basic text for the student

Philip J. King. *The Book of Judges.* New York: Paulist Press, 1960.

Specific objectives

I. To give the student a brief view of the post-Josue consolidation of Canaan during the twelfth and eleventh centuries B.C., to the establishment of the monarchy.

II. To present this period of the history of the Israelites under the apsect of God's leadership of them through the national heroes whom He elected, the so-called judges.

III. To clarify the concept of these heroes, so that they come to be known to the student, not as judges, but as charismatic leaders divinely elected as the agents through whom He would act in guiding the consolidation of the tribes of Israel. They were not only men of their times, but they were leaders who were not perfect models of virtue. The possession of charismatic gifts is not a guarantee of holiness.

IV. To unify the incidents recorded in the sacred text in the light of the rhythmic pattern of rebellion of the Israelites and their return: apostasy from Yahweh; oppression of Israel by her enemies; her return to Yahweh by repentance; Yahweh's election of a charismatic leader to bring Israel victory over her enemies.

V. To develop the student's notion of "history" as it is found in the Bible. History as a literary form among the Semites and other ancient oriental peoples is *not history in our modern sense;* the author of the sacred text was not concerned and did not even know the essentials of the historical method demanded by the contemporary historian. He wrote history in the popular, anecdotal style characteristic of the ancient Near East. The Book of Judges, perhaps, can best be used to clarify this concept in the mind of the student, so important in contemporary situations if he is to answer intelligently the position of those who deny the historicity of the Scriptures, as well as those others who confuse the theological history of salvation with scientific history as such.

VI. To emphasize through the recurring cycle of apostasy, oppression, repentance, deliverance around which the anecdotal stories of the national heroes is constructed, the revelation which God makes of Himself through His divine plan in executing His acts of intervention in behalf of the people of Yahweh: His justice and holiness by punishing their sin; His mercy in forgiving the repentant; His omnipotent goodness in saving the oppressed. This insight is important for future study of theology, if the student is to see that what is called "the divine pedagogy" is operative in every period of the history of God's governance of the universe and His plan of salvation.

VII. To develop the student's concepts regarding morality in the Old Testament; to enlarge his view of the gradual progress in moral standards in the Bible; to deepen his awareness of the effects on moral judgment of the milieu in which men live their lives and with the further realization of the consequent obligation of the people of Yahweh to witness to God's Law.

The purpose of this unit can best be attained by a careful study of the commentary on the part of the student, supplemented by explanations, especially of the areas listed above, by the instructor. Time for this unit should be kept at a minimum in the total course.

Suggested directives for student's thought, reading and study

1. Be prepared to discuss intelligently with a student who is majoring in history, but who may not have had the opportunity to study Sacred Scripture as you have had, the differences in the concept of "history" as it is understood by the modern American, and the concept of "meditated history" as the term is understood by the people of the ancient Near East and by the author of the Book of Judges.

2. Justify the statement: "The Judges are primarily *inspired military leaders* raised up by

God to deliver His Chosen People from domination by their enemies."

3. From your study of the Deuteronomic tradition and its characteristics as you studied them in Deuteronomy, have you been able to recognize certain aspects of Judges which could be classified as belonging to this tradition? What are they?

4. Explain the following statement in the light of your study of Judges: "The Former Prophets, speaking under inspiration, gave the revelation of what God expected of His people, what He received in response, and how, despite a pitiful response to His love and guidance, He did not abandon them, but continued patiently to correct their aberrations and to lead them in His own way to the fulfillment of their destiny."

5. Recall God's covenant promises made to Israel. In return for fidelity to the covenant, God had promised peace and prosperity; in return for infidelity, oppression and punishment. Observe how this teaching is explicitly formulated in Judges 2 and then exemplified in the history of the twelve judges in Judges 3-6. Note that these covenant promises are made in terms of the temporal. Have you ever considered what an evidence of God's mercy it was that He did not reveal in any clear idea the nature of eternal reward in the Old Testament? Admission to an eternal reward was a long way off! All those pre-Christian centuries must pass before Heaven and the Beatific Vision could be attained.

Watch for the development of the concept of future reward in your subsequent study in this course.

6. Read the Book of Ruth for a delightful picture of the life of a faithful Israelite family set in the midst of the rude, barbaric age of the "Judges." It is the story of David's great grandmother. Ruth, a Gentile, is the heroine whose narrative gives an interesting insight into son or daughter-in-law relations in married life. More importantly, however, the book has a more pertinent revelation, namely, the universality of God's call to salvation by showing how even a Gentile like the Moabitess, Ruth, could be called by God to enter the genealogical line of the Messiah (cf. Matt. 1:3-6; Luke 3:31-33). Watch in your study the development of this concept of universal salvation as it opens up.

7. In regard to the Book of Judges, explain the meaning of the following statement: "The Bible is a book of life and, without necessarily approving the deeds of its characters, it presents them as flesh and blood individuals who, at times, were large vessels of clay (II Cor. 4:7). Nevertheless God used such men in His plan of salvation."

Eighth Unit - The Institution of the Israelite Monarchy and its Perpetuity in the Dynasty of David from which One Day Will Be Born the Messiah

Indicated passages from the Books of I and II Samuel are to be read by the student.

The outward form of the kingdom of God changes with the introduction of the monarchy, but its essence perdures; while acceding to the will of His chosen people for an earthly king, Yahweh still rules His people; the divine promise to Israel that the dynasty of David will be eternal and that through this dynasty God will work out the victory of mankind promised in Genesis 3:15.

Summary of the historical background for the study of this unit

I. I Samuel, the last of the Judges, constrained by the demands for a king of the oppressed Israelites who are envious of the independence of their neighbors, the Moabites and Edomites, with their hereditary kings and standing armies, against his will accedes to their will. He chooses Saul the Benjaminite.

    Cf. A. I Samuel 1-7 for the account of the Philistine oppression which moves Israelites to demand a king; note the following passages for the history of Samuel, the Judge: 1:11; 2:1-10; 3:1-4:1.

B. Note the typical theological pattern of Judges in I Samuel 7:2-14.

II. Institution of the monarchy:

   A. Summarized in I Samuel 7:15-17.

   B. Two versions fused:

      1. The antimonarchist version in I Samuel 8; 10:17-24; 12: God alone is Israel's true king; cf. Deuteronomy 17:14 ff.

      2. The promonarchist version in I Samuel 9:1-10:16; 11.

   C. Saul is anointed king by Samuel only privately at first (10:1); and later after his victory over the Ammonite, publicly (11:1-15).

   D. Samuel's speech in 12:13-25; the demand for a king has displeased God, but if the king will listen to God's prophet and obey, God will continue to watch over His people (cf. Deut. 17:14-20).

   E. Saul's failure to obey God's prophet (to await Samuel at Gilgal) brings about his rejection (13:8-14; 15:10-35; two versions of the same disobedience). Note: "Does the Lord delight in burnt offerings and sacrifices as much as in obedience to the voice of the Lord? Behold to obey is better than sacrifices and to hearken, than the fat of rams" (15:22).

   F. The interesting history of Saul and David (I Sam. 16:31).

III.   A. David, King over Judah after the death of
       Saul (II Sam. 1-4). Note: David's elegy la-
       menting the deaths of Saul and Jonathan!

       B. David, king over all Israel and nearby con-
       quered nations (II Sam. 5-20).

           1. David conquers Jerusalem by stratagem
              and makes this ancient Canaanite city
              his new capital (II Sam. 5:6-9).

           2. He consolidates his position as king of
              all Israel by bringing the Ark of the
              Covenant to Jerusalem, making it the
              religious as well as the national capital.

           3. Nathan's prophecy (II Sam. 7:1-16) to
              David of an eternal dynasty; in return
              for the material house for God which
              David would have built, God promises
              to David a "house," a royal house, a
              dynasty that will endure eternally.

              Stress here that "house" and "seed"
              are to be taken in a collective sense;
              cf. Isaias 9 for the further confirma-
              tion of this promise; Psalm 88:30-38;
              Luke 1:32 ff; Apocalypse 11:15.

           4. Brief summaries of the Davidic period
              of kingship found in II Sam. 8:15-18;
              20:23-26 are pertinent; the finale of the
              court history of David (II Sam. 9-20;
              III Kings 1-2).

IV. The reign of Solomon.

       A. Solomon's accession to the throne (III
       Kings 1:1-2:46).

B. Solomon's divine gift of wisdom! (3:5-15).

C. Construction of Solomon's Temple in Jerusalem, the first permanent edifice dedicated to the one, true God in His universe! (III Kings 5:1-9:14). The Temple of Solomon which replaced the Tabernacle and the Meeting Tent should be emphasized in this unit, and clearly distinguished in the student's mind from the Post-exilic Temple, and likewise from the one erected by Herod which was still in the process of construction during the life of Christ. ("The Hawlings Rawley Reconstruction of the Temple of Solomon" is available in either one black and white, or one colored film strip, with an accompanying script and an illustrated booklet. Cf. *Harvard Archeological Review.*)

D. Solomon's marriages with foreign wives (perhaps for political reasons) lead him to compromise his beliefs; he builds pagan temples for his wives even in Jerusalem (11:1-10); punishment for his infidelity will be the division of the Kingdom of Israel.

E. Solomon's death (III Kings 12:2).

F. The division of the United Kingdom of Israel effected through the secession of the rebel Northern Kingdom (often called the Kingdom of Israel in contradistinction to the Kingdom of Juda, the Southern Kingdom) under Jeroboam (III Kings 12 ff).

G. The history of the Northern Kindgom (926-721 B.C.), in regard to this course, will be treated under the ninth unit: The Prophets of the Northern Kingdom in the Late Seventh and Early Sixth Centuries.

For the convenience of the students, the following historical summary of the period is included:

The Northern Kingdom of Israel possessed extensive territory and embraced ten of the original tribes of Israel; the monarchy was less firmly rooted than in the south; the tribes were not closely united; uprisings against the nineteen kings who ruled during the 200 years of the existence of this kingdom; the kings were often the victims of revolts, conspiracies, assassinations; kingdom had no authentic center for the worship of Yahweh; its capital was at Shechem; two sanctuaries were set up for worship: one at Bethel in the southern part of the kingdom, and one at Dan in the north; many false elements were introduced into the worship of Yahweh; under Achab (874-853) through the influence of his wife Jezebel, the cult of Baal became the official religion of the court and the ruling class became paganized; the false prophets of Baal and Astarte enjoyed official status; the followers of Yahweh were oppressed; God sent the prophets Elias and Eliseus to Israel to be His spokesmen; Jeroboam II (783-743), one of the most successful rulers of the Northern Kingdom, restored it briefly to some degree of apparent prosperity, but its social, moral, and religious decay had penetrated deeply and were the cause of its ultimate extinction; although Yahwism remained the national religion, many of the people gave only lip service to the covenant; covenant law meant little in practice; the prophecies of Amos and Osee were not heard; lacking internal cohesion and religious strength, the Northern Kingdom finally fell to the Assyrians in 721 B.C. The Israelites were deported to the region of Upper Mesopotamia and Media where they ultimately lost their identity as Israelites. The former kingdom of Israel was repopulated with colonists from Babylon, Elam, and Syria.

H. The history of the Southern Kingdom, the Kingdom of Juda (931-587) will be treated in regard to this course in Units Ten and Eleven. No attempt will be made to treat historically the events of the some four hundred years before Juda's capture by Babylonia in 587 B.C., and its subsequent exile.

Note: Students may be directed to evaluate certain pertinent modern films and to show how the salvation history element is omitted in such productions as those featuring the Ten Commandments, David and Bathsheba, Sodom and Gomorrah, and Ruth, etc.

Ninth Unit – The Prophets of the Northern Kingdom in the Late Seventh and Early Sixth Centuries

Basic text for the student

Marcian Strange, O.S.B. *The Books of Amos, Osee and Michea.* New York: Paulist Press, 1960. (For this unit, only the sections of the text devoted to *Amos* and *Osee* will be studied. *Michea* will be studied with *Isaia* relative to the Southern Kingdom.)

Supplementary readings for the student

J. Chaine. *God's Heralds.* Translated by Brendan McGrath. New York: Joseph Wagner, 1955.

Joseph Dheilly. *The Prophets.* Translated by Rachek Attwater. New York: Hawthorn Books, 1962.

Ignatius Hunt. *Understanding the Bible* (Chapter 18). New York: Sheed and Ward, 1962.

John McKenzie, S. J. *The Two-Edged Sword* (Chapters 2, 8, 9, 10, 11). Milwaukee: Bruce, 1956.

Frederick L. Moriarty, S.J. "The Prophets: Bearers of the Word," *The Bridge*, III, 1958-1959.

Paul Synave, O.P., and Pierre Benoit, O.P. *Prophecy and Inspiration.* New York: Desclee, 1961.

Bruce Vawter, *The Conscience of Israel.* New York: Sheed and Ward, 1961.

Suggested sources for the teacher

Anderson Bernhard and Walter Harrelson, eds. *Israel's Prophetic Heritage.* New York: Harper and Row, 1962.

L. Cerfaux *et al. L'Attente du Messie.* Paris: Desclee de Brouwer, 1954.

A. Robert and A. Tricot. *Guide to the Bible*, Vol. I (rev. ed.). New York: Desclee, 1960, pp. 340-341; 342-343.

PART I

Specific objectives

I. To introduce the student to a correct understanding of prophetism in relation to God's revelation and to the inspired text of Sacred Scripture.

Note the following distinctions:

A. "The Former Prophets," according to the Massoretic text, who wrote but did not preach: authors of Josue, Judges, Samuel, Kings; documentary sacred history used to proclaim God's revelation of Himself and His salvific acts.

B. The earlier preaching prophets who preached, but did not write: Samuel, Nathan, Elias, Eliseus; their few recorded oracles and brief sermons are recorded with historical and psychological context; e.g., Moses, in Exod. 4-19; Samuel, in I Sam. 8-15; Nathan, in II Sam. 7 and 12; Elias in III Kings 17-19; Eliseus in IV Kings 3-8.

C. The "Latter Prophets" not only preached, but put their sermons in writing for the benefit of posterity: Amos, Osee, Michea, Isaia, Jeremia, Ezechiel, Daniel, etc.; their lengthy sermons and oracles are given without immediate and precise historical context, but rather in the form of an anthology of sermons, with brief descriptions at the beginning to indicate the general period and specific kingdom in which the prophet preached, and with very meager internal evidence to indicate other circumstances of his work. These particular categories of the prophets will be followed in the units of the course devoted to prophetism.

II. To develop the true concept of "prophet": *not* men whose words were, for the most part, predictions of future destruction, or revelations about the coming Messiah and His kingdom, but men whose principal concern was the current existential situation, the events, vicissitudes, challenges to the religious life of their immediate contemporaries. They were not missionaries announcing the truths of salvation to men who had never heard them; nor were they ordinary preachers, like the priests in the Temple; but rather extraordinary preachers, men whom God inspired to preach on subjects of fundamental religious importance at times of religious crises. The prophet is God's mouthpiece, conscious of speaking not his own message, but the message God inspires him to speak, and that message may concern the past, the present, or the future.

To further clarify the concept of prophet and prophetism, the following ideas should be emphasized in the units in the course devoted to the prophets:

A. The distinction between false and true prophets:

    1. False prophets claimed to speak as God's spokesmen; the true prophet received a divine call to prophecy; cf. Moses, in Exod. 3:7-22; 4:1-15; Amos, in 7:14-16; etc., and the certitude of his own inner experience of God's will, even in face of personal repugnance to the call.

    2. True prophet is distinguished from the false by the

        a. integrity and holiness of his life;

        b. agreement of his teaching with traditional Mosaic doctrine;

        c. often, but not necessarily, he is certified by the testimony of miracles, and of prophecies fulfilled in his own lifetime.

III. To develop an understanding of the purpose of prophetism as an institution among God's people. Israel, because of the danger of syncretism with the Canaanite religions in the early centuries of her history, and subsequently because of the failure of Israel's kings and priests, was in constant need of an authoritative voice to keep alive the meaning of the covenant bond, the Mosaic covenantal bond with Yahweh, and to warn the people of God against the perpetual temptation of infidelity to Yahweh in matters of worship, morality, and that which pertained to their special vocation as a nation. Prophetism, therefore, was the divine institution whereby the prophets became the bearers of Israel's messianic hope which had been kindled by the Sinaitic Covenant and brought to a flame by the promise of David of a perpetual dynasty.

IV. To develop insights into the nature of prophecy:

    A. Its essence is a subtle divine influence upon the intellect and will of the prophet inclining him to speak those things, and only those things which God wills to be communicated.

    B. The personality of the prophet is not changed by the charismatic gift of prophecy, any more than the personality of the inspired author of Sacred Scripture is changed by the charismatic gift of biblical inspiration.

    C. But there is evidence that the prophets were conscious, to a limited extent at least, of God's influence on them; they speak of visions (genuine mystical experiences) by which God made His presence and His message experientially manifest to His prophets. (Cf. Jer. 15:16-21; 20:7-11, etc.)

D. Despite the visions and conscious experiences of divine communications, the prophet spoke without being aware of acting under inspiration. In this they are like the inspired biblical author. Both the prophet and the inspired author were conscious that they were fulfilling their divine mission by preaching or writing the things of God; they were not necessarily conscious of the divine influence on their faculties under which they spoke or wrote.

V. To develop an understanding of the characteristics of the writings of the prophets:

A. Their traditional adherence to the doctrine contained, either explicitly or implicitly, in the Mosaic Covenant with which the student has become familiar through the study of the Pentateuch and the Books of the Former Prophets.

B. The traditional doctrine is expressed with peculiar emphasis relative to the needs of the existential situation in which the prophet is speaking.

C. The traditional doctrine is presented not dialectically or apologetically, but forcefully so as to persuade to action.

D. The recurrence of easily recognizable traditional themes, standardized expressions, and the "same kind of doctrinal unanimity with regard to the Mosaic teaching as one finds among the Fathers of the Church with regard to the teaching of Christ in the Gospels."

These objectives should be pursued in each of the subsequent units on the prophets. Students could review them frequently with profit in an effort to develop understanding of the institution of prophetism in Israel.

PART II

(A Study of Amos and Osee, Prophets of Israel)

Objectives

I. Through the study of Amos and Osee to give an insight into the salvation history of the Northern Kingdom of Israel without emphasis on the complexity of detail relative to kings, etc., pertaining to this period of its history.

II. Through the study of these two books, to develop in the student a relative familiarity with the most important themes which will recur subsequently in the other prophets, and with the literary forms in which they will be expressed most frequently.

  A. Literary forms:

    1. Oracles against the nations; the traditional literary form found in prophetical writing. Cf. Amos 1-2.

    2. Visions: they are at times descriptions of genuine mystical experiences (Isa. 6); at other times they may be purely literary descriptions used as rhetorical device.

B. Themes of the prophetical writings:

1. Special favor of Yahweh implies special obligations; cf. Amos 3:2; 9:7; Osee 13:4-8.

2. Denunciation of formalism in worship; cf. Amos 4:4-5; 5:21-26; Osee 6:6.

3. Divine chastisements (war, famine, plagues, pestilence, exile) are inflicted to induce reflection, repentance, reformation; cf. Amos 4:6-13; 5:1-9; Osee 2:4-17.

4. The Day of the Lord. The expression in the prophets refers to the intervention of God in history (1) to judge and punish either Israel or Israel's enemies; (2) to bring about the messianic age; or (3) to judge the world at the end of time. Cf. Amos 5:18; 8:9; 9:11.

5. The idea of "the remnant"; there will be a few faithful Israelites who in messianic times will become the foundation of a New Israel; cf. Amos 9:8-10.

6. The idea of the messianic kingdom; the hope of Israel in the Davidic family, based on the prophecy of Nathan (II Sam. 7-12) and on the Yahwist's salvation history; cf. Amos 9:11.

7. The idea of the new paradise; descriptions of the messianic era in terms of the conditions in paradise found in Genesis 2-3; cf. Amos 9:11-15; Osee 2:19-24; 14:5-8.

8. The marriage theme; the covenantal bond between God and His people expressed in terms of the spouse relation in human marriage; cf. Osee 1-3.

9. The New Exodus; the realization of Israel's messianic hope is presented as a New Exodus from physical and spiritual captivity to a new life of intimate love for God and joyful fidelity of His will; cf. Osee 2:1-3; 2:16-25.

10. The futility of dependence on human alliances as opposed to dependence on God; cf. Osee 5:11-14; 7:8-16.

11. The idea of Israel's relation to God under the concept of sonship; God's great love for His people likened to that of a father for his child; cf. Osee 11:1-4.

Suggested directives for student's thought, reading and study

1. How does Amos use the political, social, and religious conditions of the immediate life situation in the Northern Kingdom of Israel, to proclaim as God's spokesman the divine message?

   A. Consult a map in a biblical atlas for the general location of the nations upon which Amos pronounces the judgment of Yahweh.

2. Observe carefully in your reading of the prophets, the frequent use of the expression, "Hear this word, the word of the Lord." This term

"word" in regard to revelation, biblical inspiration, and prophecy should have much deeper meaning for you as you progress in this course.

3. What are the evidences of social injustice and the violation of basic human rights prevalent in the time of Amos which he denounces in his prophecy? Is there any similarity to the conditions of our own day?

4. Amos is severe in his denunciation of the women of Israel. Why?

5. Observe in the Second Word (Amos 4:6-11), the characteristic Semitic thought pattern which has been stressed in previous areas in this course, namely, the attribution of natural effects directly to God without the recognition of secondary causes.

6. Numbers again in Amos! Can you interpret in the light of principles which you have previously learned?

7. You will find an interesting summary of the fulfillment of Amos' predictions concerning the future in the commentary on pp. 9-10, beginning with the statement: "All these promises of doom became terrible reality. . . ." Be prepared to explain the statement historically.

8. "The God of Amos is characterized by His justice, i.e., by His power to give the moral order realization on earth." Explain this statement.

9. Notice the doxologies in Amos 4:13; 5:8-9; 9:5-6. They were probably added to the original

text to serve the purpose of liturgical reading. Are these doxologies inspired then? You will find this idea of liturgical additions in the biblical text important in your study of Sacred Scripture, especially in the New Testament.

10. Compare the simple direct language and the rustic imagery of Amos with the tender beautiful imagery of Osee.

11. Amos promises a "famine upon the land; not a famine of bread, but for hearing the words of Yahweh" (8:11). What does the statement mean?

12. The historical background of the prophecy of Osee in Israel is given in the commentary, pp. 35-36. It is important that you study it carefully, if you are to understand the political conditions responsible for the ultimate destruction of the Northern Kingdom of Israel.

13. Make a careful study of the concept of "spouse relationship" used by Osee to describe Yahweh's covenantal bond with His people. Note he speaks of a new marriage between Israel and Yahweh, and foretells a day when God will lead Israel into the desert, speak to her heart, convert her, and then espouse her forever in a new covenant of right and justice, love and mercy (2:16-25). You will find this theme beautifully developed in the Canticle of Canticles. Isaias, Jeremia, and Deuteronomy, each uses the same theme; St. Paul will also develop it in his epistles. It is worthy of your serious consideration, if you are to understand the covenant

bond between God and His people, both in the Old Testament and in the New.

14. Amos has been called the prophet of social justice; Osee, the prophet of divine love. Justify this statement by references to their respective prophecies.

15. The adultery of Israel spoken of by Osee is allegorical, representing religious infidelity to Israel's covenant-vowed monotheism. Notice how often this allegory is used by the sacred authors in the bible in regard to the Israel of God.

16. From your study of Amos and Osee, discuss the significance of the following statement: "The Prophets never cease to be relevant. We need to read the prophets, *not* in order to see if we can figure out data about the future of the world and man, but in order that we may better know and become sensitive to the will of God."

Tenth Unit - The Prophets of the Southern Kingdom of Juda in the Late Seventh and Early Sixth Centuries

Basic texts for the student

The commentary and text of the Book of Michea in *The Books of Amos, Osee, and Michea.* New York: Paulist Press, 1960.

John E. Huesman, S.J. *The Book of Isaia,* Part I. New York: Paulist Press, 1960.

Supplementary readings for the student

Those listed under ninth unit.

Suggested sources for the teacher

Cf. bibliographies under ninth unit.

Objectives

I. To continue to develop understanding of the concept of prophetism according to the objectives listed under the previous unit.

II. To give insight into the salvation history of God's chosen people in the Kingdom of Juda.

Suggested directives for student's thought, reading and study

Concerning Michea

1. Read carefully the passages in the Book of Michea in which he describes his prophetic mission: Michea 3:8; 7:7. Compare with pas-

sages in Amos and Osee which are expressions of their vocation.

2. Note carefully the passages in Michea in which the historical details relative to the background of his preaching are stated: 1:1; 1:8-16. (The following passages from other books of the Old Testament are important insights into his prophetical mission and achievement: IV Kings 18:3-6; II Chron. 29:8-11; Jer. 26:18-20).

3. Compare the historical background against which Michea preached in the Southern Kingdom with those against which Amos and Osee preached in the Northern Kingdom.

4. Read carefully Michea 4-5; observe his prophecy concerning the future messianic "day of the Lord" when the expected Messiah will come in person and rule not only Juda, but all the nations of the world. Watch for indications in your reading and study of this note of "universalism" in regard to salvation which is gradually developed in the Old Testament. Set this idea against that of the divine election of God's chosen people from among all the peoples of the ancient world.

5. Note Michea's definition of true religion as he states it in 6:8. Explain its implications in the light of what you have studied in this course concerning God's revelation to man.

6. Michea 1:2-7 is identified by biblical scholars as a literary theophany. What is the meaning of this term? Compare this passage with the following literary theophanies: Psalms 49; 74.

7. Observe in Michea the theme of "the remnant," so characteristic of the prophets. Cf. Chapter 4.

8. Observe the dramatic trial scene of 6:1-8 in which the prophet portrays God arraigning and convicting His people of base ingratitude. It is the passage which inspired the chant known as the *Popule meus, quid feci tibi* . . . (My people, what have I done to you? . . .) which is found in the liturgy of Good Friday. Consult your Missal and read this beautiful and poignant reproach there.

9. In the light of your previous study of Michea, and that of your previous reading and study in this course, explain the following passage which occurs in the commentary, p. 72, "From time to time there seems to have been additions to this book made by inspired hands and inserted into the original collection of the prophet's speeches. These passages are found in Michea 2:12-13; 4:1-3; 4:10; 5:8; 5:14; 7:8-10; 7:11-13; 7:14-20." In reading these passages can you find any reason why they are so identified? Explain the meaning of this passage from the commentary in the light of your understanding of the extent of inspiration in regard to the authorship of the sacred text.

10. Note the prediction of the destruction of Jerusalem in Michea 3:12: If you will confer Jeremias 26:18-19, you will find that the latter prophet refers to the message of Michea as a threat which was not carried out because the conditions for escaping it were fulfilled. What important principle concerning the interpreta-

tion of prophetical predictions is illustrated here?

11. Observe carefully the explanation of the commentator on the use by St. Matthew 2:2-6, and St. John 7:42 of Michea 5:1. An important principle of biblical interpretation is cited here. Explain it in the light of the understanding of inspiration relative to this principle which you have thus far studied.

Concerning Isaia

1. Study carefully the historical background against which the prophet Isaia preached "the word of the Lord." An excellent summary for the purposes of this course is found in the commentary on Isaia, pp. 5-6.

2. Select passages from Isaia 1-39 which illustrate most adequately his essential themes:

    A. Yahweh is King, the Holy One, the Strong and powerful One.

    B. Despite the moral softness, the greed and sinful indulgence of the leaders of Juda, Yahweh will save a remnant of His people.

    C. The promised Messiah will be a King of the Davidic dynasty, a King of universal justice and peace, who will spread the knowledge of Yahweh Himself.

3. Consult the characteristic themes of the Old Testament prophecies as they are listed under the objectives in Unit Nine for the study of Amos and Osee. Observe carefully as you study

Isaia, passages which illustrate these themes in the writing of this prophet.

4. Observe the deepened insights into the nature of Yahweh as He is revealed in Isaia:

   A. Isaia's overwhelming realization of the sanctity of Yahweh which may be traced to the revelation which was given him on the occasion of his call to the prophetic office: cf. Isaia 6:1-13; 1:4; 5:19; 5:24; 10:17; 20.

5. The Book of Emmanuel, Isaia 7:1-12:6, is a very important section for thought and study. Observe carefully the commentator's explanation of the fact that God, who is the principal author of Scripture, can at times intend a meaning which goes beyond the understanding of His human instrument, the inspired author. This is the first time in the course that you have been introduced to what biblical scholars call the "fuller sense." Note the principles by which this "fuller sense" can come to be known subsequently in later centuries. Watch for other references to the "fuller sense" as you progress with this course.

6. "To the prophet it is eminently clear that it is God, and God alone, who governs the world with all its historic events. When, to remind His people that they have abandoned Him, God decides to punish them, He chooses their bitterest enemies, the Assyrians, as the rod of His anger." Explain this passage not only in regard to the history of Juda, but its implica-

tions in regard to the historical events of any other period of history.

7. Read carefully both the text of Chapter 11 and its commentary. Observe the gradual evolution of the revelation of the Messiah's person and His reign. Compare this chapter in regard to the delineation it gives of the Messiah with that presented in II Samuel 7:8-16. Read also Chapter 9 of Isaia and note the virtues of the Messiah as they are emphasized there.

8. Chapter 11:6-9 of Isaia is identified as a parable by bilibcal scholars. Have you met this literary form anywhere in your previous study of the Bible? What are the characteristics of a parable?

9. In Isaia 24:1-27:13 you meet for the first time in this course what is identified as the apocalyptic literature of the Old Testament. You will meet more frequent examples of this literary form in the subsequent units of the course. This form is frequently used by the inspired writers to present in highly poetical and figurative language the concept of the "Day of the Lord" which is to come in the future. Man's sinfulness has brought God's chastisement and the earth shall be desolate, but the destruction will be not absolute; the faithful "remnant" will remain. Just as in the creation account of Genesis God was triumphant over chaos, so too on the future Day of Yahweh He will once again assert His might over sin and death.

10. Compare and contrast the Song of the Vineyard in Isaia 5:1-7 in which Yahweh sings of the unresponsiveness of His beloved, the House of Israel, with Isaia 27:2-6 in which Yahweh's vineyard is assured of His Protection, despite its infidelity. Watch for the recurring theme of the vineyard in subsequent readings in both the Old and the New Testament. (Cf. Osee 10:1; Jer. 2:21; 5:10; 6:9; 12:10; Ezech. 15:1-8; Mark 12:1-12.)

11. Explain the following quotation from the commentary in the light of the principles you have learned in this course regarding God revealing Himself through His acts, and His Word spoken through His inspired writers and the prophets: ". . . the prophet woefully reminds his adversaries, who have spurned God's Word, that Yahweh's message wil soon come to them in another, more intelligible form—in the form of invading Assyrian hordes." Cf. 28:7-22.

12. Compare Isaia's denunciation of the social injustices of his day with that of Osee, and of Amos.

13. Read carefully Chapters 36-37. The dramatic account of Sennacherib's invasion of Juda and siege of Jerusalem in 701 B.C. is described not only in the Bible, but also in *Sennacherib's Annals*. The raising of the siege following the prediction of Isaia, left in Jewish minds the conviction that Jerusalem was impregnable and indestructible because of God's dwelling in its

midst. Read in *Ancient Near Eastern Texts*, No. 288, the account from Sennacherib's annals. (Read also Ps. 45, 47, 75; and Jer. 7:1-10 concerning the same theme.)

14. Someone has written that the Isaian slogan may be summed up in the phrase, "Believe or perish!" Absolute confidence in God and steadfast loyalty to Him is the mark of a true believer. How has the study of Isaia deepened your concept of faith in relation to God's word?

Eleventh Unit - The Judean Prophets during the Last Hundred Years of the Kingdom

Basic texts for the student

Edward J. Crowley, C.SS.R. *The Books of Lamentations, Baruch, Sophonias, Nahum, and Habacuc.* New York: Paulist Press, 1960.

Selections from the Book of Jeremias.

For this unit of the course, the student should follow the sequence listed below in reading the prophets of this period. The objective of this unit is to give the student insight into the salvation history of God's chosen people in the last hundred years of the existence of the Kingdom of Juda as it is uttered in the prophecies selected for study.

Sophonias: In the last years of the Southern Kingdom, the voice of Sophonias is raised in a vain attempt to prevent the onrush of national disaster, as those of Amos and Osee had been raised in the last years of the Northern Kingdom. The commentary carefully read will give the student sufficient help in understanding the text of the prophecy, in view of his familiarity with the characteristic prophetical themes explained and discussed in the ninth and tenth units.

Nahum: This prophecy should portray for the student the period of the conquest of Assyria by the Medes and Babylonians when God intervenes in favor of the oppressed satelite nations, among them Juda, and frees them from the tyranny of this hated tyrant. Nahum's prophecy is a song of triumph expressing the joy of these people. The commentary provides adequate explanation of the sacred text.

Habacuc: This prophecy is an outcry against the apparent injustice of God in allowing Babylonia, in 605, to take over the reigns of empire and oppress Juda. Habacuc poses the question which troubles him greatly: where is the justice in a sinful nation being punished by a still more sinful nation, itself deserving of punishment? God's answer comes in 2:2-4 when in a vision He tells Habacuc that "the rash man has no integrity, but the just man, because of his faith, shall live."

Jeremias: From text of Bible.

Suggested directives for student's thought, reading and study

1. Note in the introduction of the commentary, the account of the Temple of Sophonias time, the abominations of the Canaanites: infant

sacrifice, idol worship, sacred prostitution, sorcery, and divination. Cf. Chronicles 33 and IV Kings 21 for a fuller account of this background for the prophecy.

2. Observe that Sophonias is a prophet of justice and prepares the way for Jeremias, as John the Baptist will later prepare the way for Christ.

3. Observe that the preaching of Sophonias had some effect upon the Judeans, since it effected a reformation of religion and morals under King Josias; but that it was ultimately ineffective in view of the fact that Juda fell to the invading armies of Babylonia when the "Day of Yahweh" arrived for Juda.

4. From your reading Nahum, show how the whole prophecy is an oracle against one nation, Assyria. Nahum's voice is raised under inspiration to describe the fate of those who misuse their God-given power to abuse nations, destroy peoples, and inflict injustice.

5. Through a careful reading of the commentary on Habacuc, be prepared to discuss both the unique themes of the prophecy, and the particular literary devices used for the communication of the prophet's message.

6. Observe that Jeremias' prophetic activities extend from around 650 B.C. until about 580, and for the most part in Jerusalem, except for the last few years of his life which he spent in Egypt. It spans the conquest of Juda by the Babylonians in 587, and the deportation of God's chosen people into the Babylonian Exile.

7. Notice Jeremias' unwillingness to assume the prophetic office; the scorn, contempt, and hatred which he suffered, even from his relatives; the apparent futility of his preaching. Can you see in all this the reason why the Fathers of the Church regard Jeremias as a type of the suffering Saviour? As you read the prophecy, watch for the resemblance between his sufferings and those of Christ.

8. Observe not only the traditional aspects of Jeremias' preaching: the love of Yahweh, the desire of God for justice and holiness, the preparation of the remnant, and the advent of the Messiah; but likewise the unique aspects of his preaching: his emphasis on the practice of religion in spirit and in truth; the making of a future new covenant between God and Israel to replace the broken Sinai Covenant; his emphasis on the conditional nature of God's threats; and the freedom of man's will.

9. What is the significance of that phrase so often used by Jeremias in his prophecy: "Harken ye to the voice of the Lord"?

10. If you examine the following passages they will give you great insight into the soul of Jeremias. These passages are often called the "Confessions" of Jeremias: 11:18-12:6; 15:10-21; 17:12-18; 18:18-23; 20:7-18.

11. The book of Jeremias poses many problems for the commentator because of the chronological confusion that is evident in its incidents. This confusion is explained by scholars as the result

of the fact that the book contains several collections of Jeremias' sermons and biographical sketches of his life which were placed end to end, for the most part, instead of being edited into one chronologically ordered whole. What insights into the meaning of inspiration are necessary to understand how such irregularities could be possible in the sacred text of which God is the principle author?

12. Read carefully Jeremias 11:1-17. Around 621 B.C., some time after the beginning of the reformation of religion and morals undertaken by Josias, an ancient book of the Law (probably Deuteronomy or a part of that book) is found in the Temple at Jerusalem and occasioned a solemn renewal of the Sinai Covenant throughout Juda. (Cf. IV Kings 22:3; 22:8; II Chron. 34:8 ff; Deut. 27-29.)

13. Read carefully the following parables in Jeremias:

   A. The parable of the "linen loincloth" (13:1-11); it is perhaps Jeremias' first clear intimation of the Babylonian exile; biblical exegetes find it difficult to determine whether this is a literary parable, or a parable in action.

   B. The parable of the "potter" (18:1-12); God's dealings with men depend on men; his threats are conditional; if there is repentance, the threats will be withdrawn.

   C. The parable of the smashed "potter's flask" (10:1-13); a parable in action dramatically symbolizing the approaching destruction of Jerusalem.

D. The parable of the two baskets of figs (24:1-10); the good figs will remain to become "the remnant" out of which a new Israel will be born.

14. Note Jeremias' letter to the exiles of 597 B.C. in 29:1-32, in which the prophet encourages them to be good subjects of Nabuchodonosor and to await the seventy years of exile, after which God will restore them.

15. Read carefully the following passage to relive something of the desolation of God's chosen people at the destruction of Jerusalem in July, 587 B.C.; Jeremias, Chapters 39; 52; IV Kings 24:18-25:30.

16. The downfall of Jerusalem, the Temple, and the kings came as Jeremias had predicted. When it came, there were at least some who understood its significance correctly, in the light of the covenant between God and His people according to which all the nation's future depended on her loyalty or disloyalty to the stipulations agreed to on Sinai. For this "remnant," the tragedy was explicable *in terms of the faith by which Israel lived.* Among this "remnant" that faith continued to live through the years of exile and was the link that joined the Israel of old to the new Israel that arose from the grave of the exile to become a nation again in 539 B.C. Can you see from this synthesis the importance of faith understood as a response of

the human person to the Word of the Divine Person, as an encounter with the living God Who speaks to men through His inspired word of Sacred Scripture, through the inspired word of His prophets, and through the events of history?

17. At this point in your course, you will better understand the following important statement: "The fateful events of the summer of 587 B.C. had a profound influence on the development of Israel's theology." During the long and painful exile from Jerusalem that followed and all that it symbolized, Israel meditated long and seriously on the deeper implications of their covenant theology; the Israelites looked forward to their messianic hopes with greater desire for fulfillment. It was during this long exile or shortly after it that Israel's inspired writers achieved substantially the Pentateuchal and Deuteronomic histories which you have studied in the earlier units of this course. Does this not throw greater light on what is meant by the phrase so often used, "meditated history"?

Twelfth Unit - The Judean Prophets of the Exile

Basic texts for the student

> John E. Heusman, S.J. *The Book of Isaia,* Part II. New York: Paulist Press, 1960.
>
> Edward F. Siegman, C.PP.S. *The Book of Ezechiel,* Parts I and II. New York: Paulist Press, 1960.

Suggested sources for the teacher

> The *Catholic Biblical Quarterly Index* contains a number of articles relative to Isaia and the other prophetical books which will be of special interest to the teacher.

Specific objectives

> I. To give familiarity with the salvation history of God's chosen people during the period of the Babylonian Exile.
>
> II. To continue to develop understanding of the institution of prophetism in Israel.
>
> III. To further deepen understanding of the concept of biblical inspiration through the analysis of the problems relative to it as they are met in the sacred text.

Suggested directives for student's thought, reading and study

> 1. Why have scholars assigned the authorship of Chapters 40 to 65 of the Book of Isaia to an

anonymous author who has come to be known as II Isaia, or Deutero-Isaia? The commentary by Father Huesman includes Chapters 56 to 66 also under the authorship of II Isaia; however, today many scholars attribute Chapters 56 to 66 to another anonymous author who is styled Trito-Isaia who is thought to have written after the exile. Watch in your readings for the reasons that are advanced in favor of the twofold vs. the threefold authorship of the Book of Isaia.

2. What is the historical background against which Deutero-Isaia preached his inspired message?

3. Why are the following themes found in Isaia 40-41, especially significant in the light of the political and social condition of God's people in exile:

   A. Yahweh will return to Jerusalem; only the Word of God will stand forever.

   B. The omnipotence of Yahweh contrasted with the impotence of earthly rulers.

   C. Yahweh reminds His people that He has chosen them to be His own: "Fear not, I am with you!" I am with you in the events of history.

4. Read carefully the following passages which are known as the Servant Songs:

   Isaia 42:1-9

   Isaia 49:1-13

Isaia 50:4-10

Isaia 52:13-13:12

The discussion in the commentary of the difficulties of interpretation of these songs again indicates the freedom which the Church guarantees to scholars in their search for objective truth. What opinion does the author of the commentary take in regard to the identification of the Servant? Perhaps in your lifetime scholars may come to some more common agreement regarding the identification. In the meantime, it is prudent to follow the opinion of one or other competent authority such as Father Huesman, the author of your text.

5. You recall the importance attached to the "Exodus theme" in the previous units of this course. What is the meaning of the term "New Exodus" as it is used in reference to Isaia 42:10-25?

6. Read Isaia 44:24-45 and discuss the implications of this passage relative to universalism vs. the particularism of the traditional Hebraic concept of salvation.

7. Note the introduction of the imagery of the spouse relation between Yahweh and Israel in 49:14-50:3; and in 61-62. Follow this symbol or analogy in the many passages in which this relationship will be expressed in subsequent books of the Bible.

8. Isaia 40-45 is often called the Book of Consolation. Select the passages which you regard as indicative of the accuracy of this title.

9. What are the infidelities of Israel which II Isaia reproves most severely in 56, 57, 59?

10. What are the specific virtues which the people of Yahweh must practice, if their worship of Him is to find acceptance? Cf. Chapter 58.

11. What attribute of God is especially emphasized in the imagery of "the Warrior God" in 63:1-6?

12. Observe carefully the explanation given in the commentary of the text (Isa. 63:7-64), in which the sacred author would seem to imply that Yahweh Himself is responsible for the sins of His people. What is the answer?

13. In reading Ezechiel, find the answer of the prophet to the questions proposed by the Israelites in exile, as to whether it was permissible or even possible to worship Yahweh in a land not His own, in the unclean land of Babylonia, to which His people had been exiled. Remember that the Semitic mind thought of land, people, and deity as inseparable from each other. This attitude will explain the reason for the Israelite question.

14. Compare the parable of the vine as you have observed it in the prophets studied in previous units with that in Ezechiel 15:1-8; 17:1-24; 19: 10-14.

15. Compare the use of the imagery of the spouse-relation in Ezechiel with its use as you have observed it in previous study of the prophets in this course.

16. The shepherd theme is a popular one with the inspired authors of the Bible. Read carefully Chapter 34 of Ezechiel and note its messianic implications.

17. What is the significance of the vision of the dry bones in Ezechiel 37:4-14?

18. Explain the characteristics of the New Israel as it is set forth in Ezechiel 40:1-48:35.

19. Ezechiel has been called the "Father of Judaism" because of the influence which his teaching exerted on the Exilic and post-Exilic communities, in placing emphasis on the *Law and Worship*. Israel was not merely a nation, but a "church," a priestly people of Yahweh. In the subsequent prophetical books which you will study during this course, watch the emphasis placed on these two important elements of Jewish life—*Law and Temple*.

20. Notice (in Ezech. 16:41-43) that Ezechiel uses the allegory of a faithless wife as an example of the infidelities of Israel toward Yahweh. Compare his allegory with others on the same theme which you have met in your study.

21. Chapters 40-43 of Ezechiel containing a lengthy vision in which the prophet speaks of the New Temple, the altar and worship, has been called the "Torah of Ezechiel." What does this mean?

Thirteenth Unit - The Post-Exilic Prophets

Basic texts for the student

Raymond E. Brown, S.S. *The Book of Daniel*. New York: Paulist Press, 1960.

Carroll Stuhlmueller, C.P. *The Books of Aggai, Zacharia, Malachia, Jonah, Joel, Abdia*. New York: Paulist Press, 1960.

Supplementary readings for the student

J. Chaine. *God's Heralds*. Translated by Brendan McGrath. New York: Joseph Wagner, 1955.

Bruce Vawter. *The Conscience of Israel*. New York: Sheed and Ward, 1961.

Specific objectives

I. To develop familiarity with the salvation history of God's Elect of Israel during the post-Exilic period.

II. To continue to develop understanding of prophetism in Israel in the period when the fulfillment of their hope for the "Day of the Lord" approaches. In order that the student may have an adequate understanding of the historical background of Israel during the last centuries of the pre-Christian era, without too great detailed study of the complexities of those centu-

113

ries, the following outline summary with designated readings should be studied:

A. The Israelites' return from the Babylonian
Exile; although under Persian control, they
are given complete religious liberty; Cyrus
is the agent elected by Yahweh to liberate
Israel through his decree of 538 B.C.; cf.
Ezra 1:2-4; 6:3-5 for the two forms of this
decree recorded in the sacred text; cf. Isaias
41:2-5; 25; 45:1-3.

B. The hostile Samaritans oppose the activities
of the returned Israelites in Jerusalem in
regard to:

1. The rebuilding of the Temple (it was
actually built in 513 B.C.).

2. The rebuilding of the walls of Jerusalem. Cf. Ezra 3-6; Nehemiah 1-6.

(The prophecies of Aggai and Zacharia
are to be set against this period.) Something of the longing of the Israelites for the
Temple can be sensed in these Psalms:
78; 73; 76; 101; 106; 136; 41-42; 83; 86.

III. Renewal of the covenant with Yahweh on the
return of the Israelites. Cf. Nehemias 9; Israel's
profession of faith which contains a recital of
the history of Yahweh's dealing with His people.

IV. Summary of the Persian Period (538-333 B.C.).

A. Hebrew was gradually replaced by Aramaic
as a language of daily living; Hebrew continued to be the language of the Law and

Liturgy, and was considered the literary or classical language. In Palestine as well as in Diaspora, Aramaic was the spoken language.

B. During this period the Old Testament, for the most part, was given its present form; the Pentateuch and the "Former Prophets" (Josue, Judges, I and II Samuel, II and IV Kings) received their final revision, and the works of the "Latter Prophets" (Isaia, Jeremias, Ezechiel, etc.) were worked over. How long that "meditated history" on the acts of Yahweh for His People had been in the writing! (During this period, in general, the prophecies of Malachia, Abdia, and Joel will be set.)

V. Israel under Hellenistic Influence.

A. With the conquest of Persia by Alexander the Great, Israel comes under Hellenistic influence. Many Jews settled in Alexandria, which became a center of Greek culture. The Bible was translated into Greek to meet the needs of these Jews. It is known as the Septuagint version.

B. During the Ptolemaic and Seleucid dynasties, Israel at first was granted religious liberty; the high priest continued to be the spiritual head of the community as well as its prince; but in the second century B.C., the attitude of the Seleucids changed. In 169 B.C., Antiochus entered Jerusalem, plundered the Temple, ordered it to be converted into a shrine of Zeus, and a Greek altar placed over the Jewish Altar of holocausts; he forbade the practice of the Jewish religion. The observance of the Sabbath, the possession of copies of the Torah, and the practice of circumcision were punishable by death. Many Jews became apostates, but many also suffered martyrdom because they refused to obey the decrees of Antiochus. Cf. I Mach. 2:29-38; II Mach. 6:11; 1:60-69; 6:10. This was a new period of crisis for the People of Yahweh. (Against the background of Antiochus, the book of Daniel was written.)

VI. Juda brought under Roman control in 63 B.C.

A. Herod the Great conquered Palestine and ruled it until his death in 4 B.C. In order to gain the good will of the Jews, he married one; he also began the construction of a New Temple in Jerusalem that would rival the one built after the Babylonian Exile. This is the Temple of Jerusalem in which Christ taught; it had not been completed until after His time.

Directives for student's thought, reading and study

1. It is in the Exilic and post-Exilic periods of the history of God's people that the Pentateuch and the books of the "Former Prophets" took their final form. The priests who had been in exile in Babylonia had been greatly influenced by Ezechiel. These priests instructed the people

there. They had recounted the sacred history of Yahweh's people, preserved the memory and recital of His acts of intervention on their behalf, as well as the memory of the liturgical laws and customs which had been the life of the chosen people united about the Temple of Solomon. These priests took the older accounts, systematized them, highlighted the features they considered most important. It was thus that the Priestly tradition so greatly influenced the final form of the Pentateuch in which the Yahwist, the Elohist, and the Deuteronomic materials came to be organized in one great work. It was the Priestly tradition that fashioned the first chapter of Genesis, as you recall. What insight do these observations give you regarding the composition of God's Word in the Bible?

2. Compare the following references and observe the familiar themes of the Old Testament prophets found in the New:

   A. The theme of the Good Shepherd (cf. Ezech. 34 and John 10).

   B. The theme of the vine and the branches (cf. Isa. 3:14; Osee 10:1; Ezech. 10:10-11; John 15).

3. When you study the New Testament you will find that Christ often referred to the prophets and their teachings. Perhaps even now you recall from reading the Gospels having seen frequently the expression, ". . . as was spoken by the prophet. . . ." In your use of the Missal, notice the frequent citations from the Prophets,

especially Isaias, Ezechiel, and Daniel and others with whom you have now become familiar.

4. Observe carefully the statement made by Father Carroll Stuhlmueller, C.P., in his commentary on the post-Exilic prohets, p. 7: "In the post-Exilic age, the years after 538 B.C., history had run full cycle." Study carefully the development of the implications of this statement in the pages of the commentary that follow. It will serve as a "bird's-eye" review of the course as you have followed it and give you an interesting insight into the part that lies ahead.

Concerning Aggai

1. From your reading of Aggai, justify the statement: "Aggai was a leader with a strong faith in God and a down-to-earth sense of reality; he concentrated his efforts and his message on the one practical task of rebuilding the Temple in Jerusalem.

2. Read Hebrews 12:26 and observe its relation to Aggai 2:1-9.

3. From your study of the Old Testament, construct an outline of the history of the Samaritans in order to show the reasons for their enmity toward the Jews.

4. Aggai 2:20-23 is important in the transmission of the ancient tradition (cf. II Sam. 7) that the anointed one of Israel who would come in the "Day of the Lord" would be David's son. Why does Aggai appropriate this messianic title to Zorobabel?

Concerning Zacharia

1. One of the reasons to which is ascribed the difficulty of interpreting the text of Zacharia is the fact that it has been damaged in transmission through the centuries. Is this book then, as it is found in the Bible today, an inspired book? What are the principles which will dictate a correct answer to this question?

2. Compare the apocalyptic literary form as you have found it in Ezechiel 1-2; 40-48 with that of Zacharia in 2:5-17; 3:1-10; 4:4-10.

3. Note in Zacharia 6:9-15 the recurrence of the theme of II Samuel 7 ff.

4. Compare Zacharia 7:1-3; 8:8-19 with 7:4-14 relative to his answer to the two questions proposed about fasting. What relation do his answers have to the theme that you have found so frequently in the prophets: "to worship God in spirit and in truth"?

Concerning Malachia

(Recall that the Temple in Jerusalem has been rebuilt.)

1. What are the special priestly sins and abuses which Malachia denounces? What are the social injustices of his time which he excoriates?

2. Malachia predicts a universal liturgical sacrifice. Read 1:10-12. This passage will have a special significance as you study the one universal sacrifice of the New Law.

Concerning Jona

1. Read carefully the commentary on Jona and get a "fresh breath" of insight into this story about which you may have had some misgivings and doubts previously. The commentary will indicate again the importance of identifying the literary form in which God's inspired word is expressed, if the meaning is to be correctly understood which He as principal author and its human author intended to convey.

2. Observe the reasons assigned by the author of the commentary for placing Jona among the prophets of Israel.

3. Why is Jona important from the point of view of God's teaching concerning His love for all men and His plan of universal salvation?

Concerning Second Zacharia

1. "The prophet writes about unbelievable sorrows resulting in wondrous joys." What are these sorrows and these joys of the Israel of God as they are described in the commentary?

Concerning Daniel

(The last of the Prophets of the Old Testament! Preached about a century and a half before the Christian Era.)

1. Be prepared to discuss the historical background against which the prophecy of Daniel was written. (Cf. Commentary, pp. 5-7.)

2. What are the unique features involved in the composition of the Book of Daniel? What is

their pertinence regarding the subject of biblical inspiration?

3. In discussing the languages in which the Book of Daniel was written, the author of the commentary gives interesting data concerning versions of the Bible and the Jewish, Protestant, and Catholic canons of Sacred Scripture, respectively. Ask your instructor to recommend sources for your further study of these subjects.

4. What is meant by apocryphal literature? What connection does this type of literature have in a discussion of Sacred Scripture?

5. Discuss the meaning of the three tests and the three visions of Daniel 1-6.

6. What is the meaning of Daniel 7? Observe carefully the explanation in the commentary on the title "Son of Man." This will be an important concept in the study of the New Testament. Christ frequently applies this title to Himself.

7. Lions are featured in Daniel 6:23 and Chapter 14. What is the reason in each case?

8. Observe the epistles in each of the following Mass texts in your Missal and see the importance which the liturgy attaches to the prophecy of Daniel:

Saturday of the Third Week of Lent: Daniel 13:1-9, 15-17, 19-30, 33-66.

Tuesday of Passion Week: Daniel 14:27, 28-42.

Thursday of Passion Week: Daniel 3:25, 34-45.

9. Read Daniel 3:26-45.

Summary and introduction to subsequent units in course

Throughout your study of the Old Testament you have observed frequent references to the words, "The Day of the Lord," "The Day of Yahweh," "He who is to come," "The anointed of Israel." Your attention has been specifically directed to the prophecy of Nathan (cf. II Sam. 7) and to the frequent repetition of its theme in the Latter Prophets; namely Yahweh has made a covenant with the House of David, a covenant that will last forever. The prophets when they spoke of that eternal covenant, saw it as the perfect kingdom of God to be realized in the "new David," one who like the first David, but more perfectly, would bring to fulfillment the goal of peace, justice, mercy, and piety so long desired by the Israel of God, and fulfill its hope for victory and greatness. (Cf. Ps. 109:1-3; 88:35-38; 2; Osee 3:5; Jer. 30:8-9; Ezech. 34:23-24; Isa. 9:1-6; 11:1-9; Jer. 23:1-6; Ezech. 17:22-25; 34:23-24.) Implicitly, the notion of the "new David" was the idea of a personal "anointed one."

It is important to understand the manner in which the prophet spoke of this glorious future which has come to be known as the Messianic Age.

I. They spoke of it in a fragmentary manner; none gave a complete picture of this messiah or described in detail the salvation he would effect; some spoke of this "new David" as a king; others as a prophet; others as a priest; Isaia spoke of him as the "Suffering Servant of Yahweh."

II. The prophets did not possess a clear understanding of the future messianic age, but spoke of it in terms of their own times. They suggested that there would be a profound change in the future, a new covenant that would be not merely external, but would be an inner reality. Their prophecies did not fully penetrate into the fulfillment of this new kingdom of Israel. Its revelation would be more perfectly delineated in the future. That revelation will be unfolded perfectly in the New Testament.

You have seen from your study of the Old Testament God revealing Himself, not through a series of logical propositions, but through His action in history. Through His acts you have come to understand His active presence with His people, and through His action and His presence, you have derived some understanding of His designs for man, and you have come to see something of His nature.

But larger horizons are about to be opened to you in your subsequent study of the New Testament. You will see the revelation of God in His Word Incarnate, the Son of God made man, the Word made flesh! You will come to see that the Chosen of Israel you have watched emerge and develop in the Old Testament is but the symbol of a New Chosen Israel, a supernatural people of the redeemed, the New Israel of God. The Mosaic Covenant, the Old Testament, will appear but as a shadow of the "new everlasting covenant" of the New Testament; the Mosaic Law will be but a figure of the great new law of charity; the prayerful spirit of thanksgiving of the Israel of God for the Exodus from Egypt will be caught up in the gratitude of the New Israel of God for its release from the captivity of sin and death; the Passover Banquet of the Paschal Lamb will be realized in its perfection in the Sacrifice and Sacrificial Banquet of the New Covenant.

"Israel itself was prophetic," a mystery, an earthly sign and symbol pointing to the eternal assembly of God, the true Israel, the Mystical Body of Christ and His members. That mystery will be unfolded in all its sublimity in the New Testament.

You have watched God's election of human agents chosen to preserve in memory, communicate, and transmit for all ages, both orally and in writing, His revelation of Himself to His creatures. You have come to understand His action in these human agents, both through biblical and prophetic inspiration. You have come to understand the importance of His providence operative in the oral transmission of the "mediated history" of His salvific acts. Your deepened understanding both of the content of divine revelation and its communication through the Old Testament will give you a wealth of insight into the more glorious revelation of Himself as Triune in the inspired text of the New.

Fourteenth Unit - The Revelation of Christ as Seen in the Gospel of St. Mark

Basic text for the student

Gerard S. Sloyan. *The Gospel of Saint Mark.* Collegeville, Minn.: The Liturgical Press, 1960.

Supplementary readings for the student

Francois Amiot. *The Key Concepts of St. Paul.* New York: Herder and Herder, 1962.

Gelin, Benoit, Boismard *et al. Son and Savior, the Divinity of Jesus Christ in the Scriptures.* Baltimore: Helicon Press, 1962.

John J. Heaney, S.J. *Faith, Reason, and the Gospels.* Westminster, Md.: The Newman Press, 1963.

Frank B. Norris. *God's Own People.* Baltimore, Helicon Press, 1962.

Augustine Stock, O.S.B. *Lamb of God: The Promise and Fulfillment of Salvation.* New York: Herder and Herder, 1963.

Suggested sources for the teacher

Y. M. J. Congar. *The Mystery of the Church.* Baltimore: Helicon Press, 1960.

F. X. Durrwell. *The Resurrection.* New York: Sheed and Ward, 1960.

J. P. Mackey. *The Modern Theology of Tradition*. New York: Herder and Herder, 1963.

Martimort, Jounel, Danielou *et al.* *The Liturgy and the Word of God*. Collegeville, Minn.: The Liturgical Press, 1959.

Jean Mouroux. *I Believe, the Personal Structure of Faith*. New York: Sheed and Ward, 1959.

Robert S. Pelton, ed. *The Church as the Body of Christ*. Notre Dame: University of Notre Dame Press, 1963.

Rudolph Schnackenburg. *New Testament Theology Today*. New York: Herder and Herder, 1963.

V. Taylor. *The Gospel According to St. Mark*. London: Macmillan, 1959.

Specific objectives

I. To give the student a unified view of the revelation of Christ as He is presented in the Gospel of St. Mark. For this end, the student should read carefully the text of the Gospel supplemented by that of the commentary, so that understanding of the Gospel text itself may be adequate in the light of the general objectives of the course. There should be no emphasis, however, on an exegetical study of the text, nor upon minor details of miracles, etc.

II. After this reading of the Gospel as a whole, its analysis should follow the plan of St. Mark's Gospel, as it is explained in the *Introduction* of the commentary, pp. 8-9. Stress here that this Gospel follows the particular pattern of apostolic preaching exemplified in St. Peter's sermon at Caesarea (Acts 10:36-43). Cf. also Acts 2:14-36;

3:12-26; 4:8-12; 13:16-41. An analysis of the essential theme of these sermons will bring an understanding of apostolic preaching as a source for the written Gospel and will contribute later to the student's understanding of the place of apostolic tradition in relation to the deposit of faith. The following ideas should be stressed in relation to this objective:

A. The existence in the primitive Church of a large body of oral apostolic tradition which antedated the writing of the Gospels; that while the word "Gospel" suggests the image of a book, in the first days of Christianity the Gospel was a Word that had been heard before it was preached, and had been preached before it was written: "Faith, then depends on hearing, and hearing on the word of Christ" (Rom. 10-17). During His earthly life Christ was the "sower of the Word"; after Pentecost, the Apostles were the ministers of His Word. Their preaching embraced a wider range of content than the *oral message* of Christ, for they had reacted both to His Words and to His acts under the action of the Holy Spirit who had moved them to an ever deeper understanding of what they had seen and heard.

B. The Apostles had been eyewitnesses of Christ's words and acts; this however, does not merely mean that they actually witnessed with their senses these physical events (many others did likewise), but that it was the *revealed word,* the teaching which specified the nature and the significance of these events and acts, and words of Christ; they had received the gratuitous divine gift of supernatural faith which enabled them to receive this teaching; moreover, and above all it was the unique influence of the Holy Spirit revealing to the Apostles the reality of that which they had seen and heard which made their apostolic preaching and teaching so important. Christ has sent His spirit to them with a special unique mission: "But when He, the Spirit of Truth, is come, He will teach you all truth" (John 16:12-13).

C. The influence of the primitive oral tradition from Simon Peter, the head of the Twelve, characterizes the Gospel of St. Mark which presents the actions, message, and teaching of Christ through the eyes of St. Peter. St. Mark had not been an eyewitness to these realities, but had received the data for his Gospel from St. Peter and from other sources.

D. The reality of Christ's words and acts under the action of the Holy Spirit had motivated the faith and the worship of the primitive Christian community. The preaching of this primitive community in its various forms of kergyma, catechesis, exhortation, and apologetic discussion certainly exercised a considerable influence on the periscopes collected in the Gospel of St. Mark, as they did in the other Gospels.

E. The actual need of preaching unquestionably governed the choice of the reminiscences of Jesus, which alone, from so many others, were chosen; that the interests which directed the choice also directed the literary form in which they were expressed; likewise it was such need which directed their theological expression, as well as their arrangement. The Gospels therefore are not biographies of Christ, but rather expressions of the theology of the New Covenant.

F. The Gospel is not history in the strict sense of that term, but in the sense that it records only what was historical; it produces sayings that are Semitic in form and content; the synoptic Gospels contain nothing of the speculative theology of the epistles of St. Paul and the Gospel of St. John, but they give the impression of a faithful and punctilious attachment to a tradition dating from Christ's own time, although they were not written for some thirty or forty years after His death. The Gospel of St. Mark, like those of St. Matthew and St. Luke, presents in a simple and rudimentary form Jesus Christ as the Son of God and Son of Man who came to bring salvation to men through His redeeming death.

III. The revelation for the divinity of Christ from the Gospel of St. Mark may be developed under the following topics:

A. Christ demonstrated supreme power over inanimate nature, over sick and dead bodies of men, and over evil spirits; while miracles in themselves are not proof of the divinity of the one who performs them, nevertheless the miracles of Christ are unique in their characteristics of credibility and naturalness; He exercised His power through His own magisterial authority, using a simple word or gesture which was immediately followed by its effect; He worked these wonders with sobriety and restraint and always for the higher reason of giving testimony to His mission and of winning faith in His word, and not to make men accept Him merely as a wonder worker in possession of unusual powers, but always to suggest something deeper.

IV. Points to be stressed through content of the Gospel of St. Mark:

  A. Jesus the Messiah; He was beginning a new age, the age of the Kingdom of God through the Holy Spirit; cf. Mark 2:19; 4; Matt. 12:28; 12:41 ff.; 13-16 f.; Luke 17:21.

  1. When He drove out unclean spirits, He was destroying the kingdom of Satan and setting up the Kingdom of God through the Holy Spirit. Cf. Mark 3:23-27 and parallels; Luke 10:18.

  2. His miracles brought to pass what the prophets, and Isaia in particular, had proclaimed; they accompanied and clearly indicated the coming of the Messianic Age. Cf. Matt. 11:2-6; Luke 7:18-23.

B. Jesus claimed that in His own Person and with sovereign power the messianic age of the Kingdom of God was inaugurated; this claim constitutes the very substance of the Gospel. But this would not necessarily involve in those who recognize His Messianic Kingdom a confession of His divinity, for the Messiah awaited by the leaders of official Judaism was a man, a King of David's lineage. His claim of supreme authority over the Law (cf. Mark 2:23-28); His miraculous command of nature (other men have worked miracles in this order); His insistence on unconditional faith in Himself could all be explained as the claims of a human Messiah (cf. Mark 10:47 ff). The disciples did not go further than this messianic faith at first.

C. But in the Gospels there are indications that Jesus' claims were on an altogether higher level than ordinary messianism. He revealed the notion:

   1. of a spiritual and moral kingdom of God, planted gently and growing slowly. Cf. parables in Mark 4.

   2. He claimed for Himself powers and titles which exceeded those traditionally attributed to the Messiah.

      a. He laid claim to the power of forgiving sins, a power which had always been reserved jealously to God Himself, as is shown by the reaction of the scribes on this occasion; (cf. Mark 2:10 and parallels).

b. Two titles are used in reference to Jesus which could surpass those of the Messiah of tradition: Jesus, Son of God, and Son of Man.

3. Emphasis should be placed on Mark 8:29 and its importance in achieving the climactic purpose of the first half of this Gospel. From 8:31 to 14:31, emphasize 9:1-7 and the events preparatory to the Passion of Christ and His explicit admission before Caiphas that the mighty power of God evident in His every word and deed stems from His Person (14:36); culminating in the confession of the centurion in 15:39; His glorification in His Resurrection and Ascension; and finally the apparitions of the Resurrected Christ and the living glorified Christ in Heaven.

V. The problem of the conclusion of the Gospel of St. Mark (16:9-20) should serve to introduce the student to an understanding of the role of the Church in determining what is to be included in the Canon of Sacred Scripture.

VI. In deepening the student's understanding of faith, it will be effective to emphasize St. Mark's apocalyptic approach to the subject, for he, of all evangelists, underlines the incomprehension by the Apostles and disciples of the full meaning of Christ's miracles and discourses.

Stress the fact that, before His death and glorification, profound insight into His divine Sonship is not attained. Faith in the Apostles is nourished, grows, deepens. It will be the work of the Holy Spirit at Pentecost to bring them from incipient faith to its fullness.

VII. With the study of the Gospel of St. Mark, the student should be introduced to the concept of Tradition through the development of the following ideas:

    A. The Catholic concept of Tradition comes in answer to the questions:

        1. How does Revelation, which was completed at the death of the last Apostle, reach all generations?

        2. What guarantees us that it reaches all generations in its integrity?

    B. Distinguish in Tradition between the:

        1. Objective element, a term which indicates the *truth* that is transmitted.

        2. Subjective or active element which indicates the process or *activity* by which it is transmitted.

        3. Note that these are not separate entities as such; they are separate only in theory.

    C. Apostolic Tradition is a rule of faith for the Church of all ages; it is normative for the whole future of the Church; it has been transmitted integrally, not only through

Scripture, but also by the life, preaching, and faith of the Church; furthermore there exists in the Church a divinely commissioned and guaranteed body of teachers to express for the members of Christ's Mystical Body the content of this Apostolic Tradition.

D. This whole apostolic deposit properly so called, i.e., the truth that came to the Church by word of mouth together with the Scriptures, is handed on in the Church and by the Church as a living Body, but particularly by the perennial Magisterium which succeeds to the functions of the mission to "teach all men whatsoever I have commanded you. . . ." Nor is this transmission a mere mechanical continual reference to truths once received, but it involves insight, clarification, and development of the meaning of the reality revealed such as the Apostles themselves would have provided had they lived in the succeeding generations of the life of the Church.

E. This Tradition is a doctrinal dispensation in the Church that brings the faith to men; the Apostles enjoyed an illumination from the Holy Spirit by which they saw the truth unfold before them in the Person of Christ. Their successors are not so favored, but their infallibility as a body is the same as that of the body of the Apostles, and the infallibility of their head is a personal infallibility similar to that which individual

Apostles had. The teaching of their successors has the same authority as that of the Apostles. Their activity, like that of the Apostles, is active Tradition; the Revelation they transmit is the objective element.

F. The whole deposit of Revelation was transmitted to the Church independently of the writing of Scripture and has been transmitted by the preaching, teaching, and practice of the whole Church, since the Apostles were commissioned by Christ to communicate the truth committed to their care. An oral deposit was thus constituted and transmitted in ways other than Scripture. This deposit is the complete corpus of revealed truth borne by the bearers of Tradition and in itself something other than their possession of, or their understanding of the Scriptures.

G. Scriptures resulted from the activity of men who were agents in Tradition, but not from their activity precisely as agents in Tradition. The writers of Holy Scripture were instruments in the hands of the Holy Spirit in such a way that He is the principal author of the works they produced. They are instruments of the Holy Spirit in a way that bearers of Tradition as such are not. The Scriptures are part of the apostolic deposit, but Scripture itself in its composition was not strictly part of the active tradition of the Apostles. In its continued documentary existence, it is the "record of

Inspiration rather than a record of Tradition, as such." Yet Scripture exercises a more important place in the living Tradition than any of the actual documents of Tradition. Scripture contains in written form the first and deepest insight into the deposit of Revelation from those who received it whole and entire.

H. But Scripture must be read in the light of the faith of the Church, for otherwise, neither the whole of inspired Scripture can be known as such, nor can much of its content be understood clearly. Both Scripture and Tradition react on each other; each perfects the other organically. But the Church is the immediate rule of Faith.

Suggested directives for student's thought, reading and study

1. Review the characteristic themes of the prophecies which you have studied in previous units, and determine which specific ones you find developed from the point of view of fulfillment in the Gospel of Saint Mark.

2. Cf. Mark 14:36 and Exodus 3:14. Why is this comparison significant?

3. The author of your commentary states that the theme of St. Mark's Gospel is: "Jesus is a Jew who acts like God." From the actions and words of Christ as they are presented in the Gospel, justify this statement.

4. Explain the following statement: "The core of this Gospel is *Kerygma*, the apostolic proclamation that Jesus who worked miracles and was crucified has risen from the dead and is now *Lord* and *Christ*."

5. Compare John the Baptist as he is presented in the Gospel of St. Mark with the prophets whom you have previously studied.

6. Study the account of the Transfiguration in Mark 9:17. Be prepared to explain its significance in relation to "the glory which Christ had from the beginning" and to a foreshadowing of that which shall be His when He fulfills His mission. What ideas learned previously from your study of the Old Testament are of help to your understanding of the text in which this event is recorded in St. Mark? Explain the possible twofold significance of the appearance of Moses and Elias with Christ at His Transfiguration.

7. Suppose yourself to be a faithful Jew living at the time that St. Mark wrote his Gospel. What would you see in his account of the Transfiguration (9:1-7) significant of the universal restoration in the "Day of the Lord" about which the prophets had written?

8. Compare the approbation of Jesus expressed by the Father in Mark 9:6-7 with that at His Baptism in Mark 1:10-11. What is the significance of these two passages in the light of Deuteronomy 18:15?

9. In regard to Mark 12:35-37, explain the following statement: "Christ won over the mass of people by His technique of revealing what must necessarily remain concealed in the very revelation."

10. Note throughout the Gospel Christ's emphasis upon loyal attachment, faith in Him, which He demands of His followers. Make a careful study of the passages therein which stress the importance of this faith.

11. Note the introduction of the concept of "the elect" in Mark 13:20. Compare this idea with the notion of "Chosen People," "the remnant," "the assembly of the people of Yahweh," with which you became familiar in the Old Testament.

12. In Mark 14:60-65, explain the significance of Christ's answers in the light of Daniel 7; in Psalm 109; and Leviticus 24:16.

13. Explain the following statement: "The final verse of St. Mark's Gospel (16:19) is, as it were, a summary of the spread of the Gospel from the glorification of Jesus as *Lord* and *Christ* down to the present day, when the chief of His signs is His Eucharistic Body and that union of charity which it achieves."

14. Explain the following statement: "The Gospel of St. Mark aims to spread knowledge of Jesus, the *Messiah* and *Son of God*, whose power is manifested by His works, and by His miracles directed to the expulsion of demons."

15. Explain the following statement in the light of your study of St. Mark's Gospel: "The core of Revelation was not the teaching of a doctrine, but the coming of a Presence among men. 'We saw his glory, the glory, as it were, of the only begotten of the Father, full of grace and truth'" (John 1:14).

16. In the light of what you have studied regarding the problem of Mark 16:9-20 in relation to the rest of the Gospel, explain the following statement: "Inspired Scripture cannot even be fully recognized as such apart from the teaching that all the books of the Canon of Scripture are inspired, a teaching which has come down to us in Tradition."

17. Explain the following statement: "The Apostles handed over to the communities which they had founded the whole content of the revelation which they had received from Christ; they handed on also their hierarchical powers to those who should follow them and lead their communities after them. The apostolic deposit or the Apostolic Tradition was placed in the Church as in a living treasury for all time. This handing over of the content of revelation was twofold: by writing and by word of mouth. The truth passed on orally is generally called Apostolic Tradition and is distinguished from Scripture. But both make up the apostolic deposit which is the source of faith from Christ for all future time."

18. A contemporary writer has said: "Faith is, of its essence, the response of the human person

to the Personal God, and is thus the meeting of two persons. In the act of faith the whole man is involved; it is the gift of the whole man. Its object is not, on the one hand, truth, and on the other happiness, but a Person who is both truth and happiness." What insight into this exposition of faith has your study of Divine Revelation through Sacred Scripture given you?

19. From your study of this course, explain the following statement: "Faith is not only the affirmation and the acceptance of a set of formulae or propositions, but a loyal attachment to Christ Himself, His mission and His work in an interpersonal communication."

Fifteenth Unit - The Primitive Church
Seen through *The Acts of the Apostles*

Basic text for the student

Neal M. Flanagan, O.S.M. *The Acts of the Apostles.* Collegeville, Minn.: The Liturgical Press, 1960.

Supplementary readings for the student

See bibliographies of previous units.

Maurice B. Schepers, O.P. *The Church of Christ.* Englewood Cliffs, N. J.: Prentice-Hall, 1963.

Suggested sources for the teacher

Andre de Bovis. *What Is the Church?* New York: Hawthorn Books, 1961.

Lucien Cerfaux. *The Church in the Theology of St. Paul.* New York: Herder and Herder, 1962.

Jean Danielou. *The Presence of God.* Baltimore: Helicon Press, 1960.

C. H. Dodd. *Apostolic Preaching and its Developments.* New York: Harper, 1936.

Philip L. Hanley, O.P. *The Life of the Mystical Body.* Westminster, Md.: Newman Press, 1961.

C. Journet. *The Church of the Word Incarnate.* New York: Sheed and Ward, 1955.

Emile Mersch. *The Theology of the Mystical Body.* St. Louis: Herder, 1951.

Pius XII. *Mystici Corporis.*

Specific Objectives

I. To give students through a careful study of The Acts of the Apostles and the commentary, an understanding of the following basic concepts important for the subsequent study of theology:

   A. A deeper insight into what may be called the "Christological kerygma," the messianic activities of Christ through His life, death, resurrection, ascension and glorification, and His Second Coming; the proclamation by the Apostles that Jesus has risen and is *Lord* and *Saviour*.

   B. To develop a deeper understanding of the concept of the Christ of history who is now the Lord of Glory whose Body, the Church, is the external manifestation of His active vivifying presence among men.

   C. To give insight into the meaning of the salvific action of the Resurrected Glorified Christ continued in the Church, His Mystical Body, made visible through the ministry of His Vicar, the Supreme Pontiff, the episcopate and the priesthood as instruments through whom Christ teaches, governs, sanctifies the New Israel of God, His Chosen People of the New Covenant.

   D. To develop understanding of this New Covenant and its terms.

   E. To give insight into the spiritual, as well as the temporal external structure of the Church in primitive Christianity as the Kingdom of Yahweh promised by the Prophets with its own constitution and its Law of charity.

F. To give insight into the period of transition of the first Palestinian community of the People of God into a universal Christianity, together with the concept of the development of Israel's faith in the Jewish Messiah into the Christian theology of the cosmic Christ, universal Saviour of all men of all times.

G. To show in the content of Acts, the existence and exercise of the functions of papacy, episcopacy, priesthood and diaconate, in regard to the institutional structure of the Church.

H. To introduce students to an understanding of the liturgical life of the New Israel of God, and its relation to the worship of the Old Testament.

I. To give a basic understanding of the Church in its function of receiving, preserving and communicating the apostolic deposit of Divine Revelation.

Suggested directives for student's thought, reading and study

1. From the text of Acts, show that the faith of the Apostles in Christ until the very day of Pentecost is incipient and imperfect, and attains its fullness under the action of the Holy Spirit; nevertheless, they are to be Christ's "witnesses to the very ends of the earth." How does

this fact indicate that God's governance of His spiritual kingdom of the New Covenant is like that of the Old, to be effected through imperfect human instruments?

2. From the text of Acts, summarize the various incidents recorded therein which clearly indicate Peter's exercise of primacy among the Apostles from the very moment of Christ's glorification. Cf. also St. Mark's Gospel.

3. In parallel columns, analyze the content of the primitive catechetical discourses recorded in Acts, and show the similarities, as well as the differences in their respective themes and development: 2:14-41; 3:12-26; 4:8-12; 5:29-32; 7:2-53; 8:30-38; 10:34-43; 13:15-41.

   A. Show how the same message of salvation is adapted in these discourses to different audiences. Note especially 10:34-43 is adapted to the Palestinian proselytes; 7:2-53 to the Hellenists; and 8:30-38 to those of the Asian diaspora.

4. Indicate the truth of the following statement: Four texts of Scripture are an evident influence on the discourses in Acts:

   A. The poems of the suffering and glorified Servant of Yahweh, particularly in Isaias 52:13; 53:12.

   B. Deuteronomy 18:15-19 describing the "prophet" like Moses whom Yahweh promises to send His people.

    C. Psalm 110:1 speaking of the Messiah as "the Lord who sits at the right hand of Yahweh."

    D. Psalm 118:22 about "the stone rejected by the builders which has become the chief cornerstone."

5. These same four texts used by the Apostles and their disciples had been used by Christ and prepared the way for the scriptural arguments for His messiahship:

    A. The Servant of Yahweh poems as the sources from which Christ drew for His prophecies of His passion and glorification: cf. Mark 8:31 and parallels; 9:31 and parallels; 10:33-34 and parallels; and Luke 22:37 compared with Mark 15:34 and parallels.

    B. He used the Deuteronomic fragment to pinpoint the nature of His work as He compared and contrasted it with that of Moses; cf. Mark 7:10 and parallels; 10:1-12 and parallels; Matt. 5:1 ff.

    C. He used Psalm 110:1 to give the theme for His discourses with the scribes about the Messiah as "Son of David" (cf. Mark 12:35-37; Matt. 22:41-46; Luke 20:41 ff.); and for the great declaration He made to the High Priest during His trial before the Sanhedrin (cf. Mark 14:62; Matt. 26:64; Luke 22:69).

    D. He quoted Psalm 118 as a last anti-Jewish thrust by way of a conclusion to the story of the unfaithful vinedressers (cf. Mark 12:10-11; Matt. 21:42; Luke 20:17).

What deductions may you draw from this data concerning the relation of the apostolic preaching to the revelations received through Christ?

6. Compare Acts 3:19-26 with 7:35 ff., and show how the following statement is implicit therein: "The ancient faithless Israel is now thrown into opposition with the new People of God, faithful and pure; Moses, the founder and law-giver of the first God-governed community has a new counterpart in Christ, the architect of the messianic assembly."

7. From your study of Acts, show the importance of the following summary: "Now in the apostolic communities, the exaltation of Christ was regarded precisely as the investiture, the enthronement of Christ as the Messiah-King. According to the most primitive teaching found in Acts (Chapter 1-10), Jesus, when 'seated at the right hand of God,' 'received' the Spirit (cf. Acts 2:32; compare 5:32 with 2:2-21). And it was under the influence and the impetus of the Spirit, that Jesus set up the Kingdom of God over whose destiny He will preside until the day of the Second Coming when His judgment will bring about its consummation (cf. Acts 10:42; 3:19-21; 4:11-12; 2:40). This coupling from the start of the Kingdom of God with the exaltation of Christ, of the Last Judgment and Parousia with the Ascension, leaves no doubt at all of the vital place which the

theme of the Messiah-King played in belief in the Lord Jesus."

8. Justify the statement that a New Covenant was promulgated on the first Christian Pentecost.

9. You have seen the effects of charismatic gifts in the governance of God's people in the Old Testament. What charismatic gifts are evident in the life of the primitive Church recorded in Acts?

10. What evidences of the sacramental principle to which your attention was directed in the Old Testament do you find in Acts? Do you observe any differences in the efficacy of these signs and symbols?

11. Miracles witness to the authority and mission of the Apostles. Explain.

12. What is the significance of the word "Church" in Acts 8:11? What concept of the Church do you derive from Acts 5:12-16?

13. Show that the key to Stephen's discourse in 7:1-53 is an understanding of the fact that as in the past God used Israel's misdeeds to further His plan for His chosen people, so too has He wrought victory through Christ's Death by His Resurrection.

14. How would you answer the charge that since Stephen's discourse is marked by seeming inaccuracies, that it cannot be divinely inspired?

15. Compare the three accounts of the conversion of St. Paul narrated in Acts 9:1-30; 22:5-21;

26:12-19. Account for the apparent discrepancies. What principles relative to inspiration are pertinent and necessary for an explanation of these discrepancies?

16. What is the singular importance of the Cornelius incident in Acts 10:1-11:18? From your study of Acts, show that the problem implicit in this incident is one which was dominant in primitive Christianity.

17. What circumstances led to the change from Jerusalem to Antioch as the center for the expansion of the Church? Why is this change important in your understanding of the Church in its primitive history?

18. What circumstances of the Council of Jerusalem (Acts 15:1-35) are of singular importance? What similarities do you see in this account with those concerning the Second Vatican Council of 1962? What are some of the differences?

19. What is the significance of Acts 15:28? Why is The Acts of the Apostles called the "Gospel of the Holy Spirit?" Cite passages to justify the title.

20. "The growth of the Church in numbers and in its own understanding of its Catholic character" may be said to be the theme of Acts 10-15. Show how St. Luke develops this theme.

21. The three missionary journeys of St. Paul as recorded in Acts 13-21 provide the historical background for the epistles which he subse-

quently wrote to several of the Churches he
established, namely, at Corinth, Ephesus, Thes-
salonica, Philippi, Rome, Galatia. When you
study these epistles later, you will find the
many parts in Acts referring to St. Paul's apostolic activities enlightening. Review a reading
of this section of Acts in the light of this later
study. The Epistles to the Colossians, Ephesians, Philemon, Philippians, as well as those
to Titus and Timothy, were written during
Paul's periods of captivity recorded in Acts 21-
28. Your reading of this section of Acts could
be directed to a better understanding of the
background in which he wrote these epistles
which you will subsequently read and study.

22. In your reading of the missionary journeys of
St. Paul, notice how frequently he stresses in
his discourses that because Jesus Christ is the
fulfillment of the promises of the Old Testament, all remission of sin must come through
belief in Him and not through observance of
the Mosaic Law. Cite passages to illustrate this
fact.

23. From your study of Acts, illustrate why St. Paul
is called the "Apostle of the Gentiles."

24. Note that the first papal encyclical is recorded
in Acts 15:23-30. What is its singular importance for your understanding of the action of
the *magisterium of the Church* in our own day?

25. How does St. Paul's text in Acts 17:22-32 differ from all others recorded therein?

26. Note the emphasis upon Christ risen and glorified which is found throughout Acts. Why this insistence rather than on the passion and death of Christ?

27. List the liturgical practices recorded of the early Christian community in Acts which you find in the practice of the Church in the twentieth century.

28. The Mosaic problem was the greatest point of irritation and difficulty in the primitive Church until after 70 A.D. Explain.

29. To profess Jesus to be "Kyrios-Lord" was an act of faith *par excellence* in the primitive Church. Why?

30. An important insight for your understanding of the Church in the twentieth century, as in the period of primitive Christianity, is contained in the following statements: "The Church manifests Christ as living Spirit. At His Resurrection, Christ entered a new way of life, a new human way of living dominated by the Spirit. Christ received the fulfillment of divine action *in His humanity* at that moment and for all eternity, so that *now* He can be called a living spirit dominated by the life-giving power of the Third Person of the Holy Trinity. The Christ who acts in and through the Church is the living Glorified God-Man, Second Person of the Blessed Trinity, the Perfect Mediator between the Heavenly Father and the New Israel, the assembly of His People, which is His Mystical Body, the Church."

Sixteenth Unit — The Church Is the People of God, the Mystical Body of Christ

Basic texts for the student

Kathryn Sullivan, R.S.C.J. *St. Paul's Epistles to Philippians, Philemon, Colossians, Ephesians.* Collegeville, Minn.: The Liturgical Press, 1960. (The Epistle to the Ephesians only is selected for special study.)

Second Vatican Council's *Constitution on the Church* and *Constitution on the Liturgy.*

Specific objectives

The study of the text of the Epistle to the Ephesians with its commentary and the *Constitution on the Church* should serve as an "overview" of the course as it has been presented, and to deepen the student's understanding of the Mystery of Christ under the particular aspect of the *Mystery of the Church, the People of God,* and *His Mystical Body,* the extension in space and time of His salvific acts unto His Second Coming!

Such an insight into this Mystery of Christ, the Mystery of the Church, should develop an understanding of the synthesis of the totality of Divine Revelation likely to induce a desire to penetrate more profoundly and specifically in subsequent courses the theology of that Mystery of His Mystical Body.

Throughout the presentation, emphasis should be placed on the necessity of faith as the total response of the whole person to God's Word spoken in this transcendent Mystery of Christ. An incipient understanding of the theology of the Word spoken and received, as it was introduced in the earlier units of the course, should be more fully developed in this unit in its presentation of the Church and its members in the totality of its dependence and theirs on Christ, the Word Incarnate.

The Mystery of the recapitulation of all things in Christ as it is set forth in Ephesians 1:3-3:21 could serve as a synthesis of the total Mystery of Christ from this introductory course to theology.

If the commentary is followed carefully, the student should attain an intelligent insight into the basic concepts implicit in the analogy of the Church as the People of God and Mystical Body of Christ of which He is the Head, and likewise of that other analogy of the epistle in which Christ is likened to the cornerstone of the Temple of the People of God.

St. Paul's analysis of the Christian (Eph. 4:1-6:20) and the text of the *Constitution on the Liturgy* may be emphasized to deepen the student's realization that the doctrine of the Mystical Body is not merely a proposition to be accepted in intellectual assent, but a truth to be loved and lived in the particular circumstances of life, personal, familial, and social.

Final Unit of the Course

As suggested in the Introduction, pp. 5-7, the final unit of study may be devoted to a reading and analysis of *Munificentissimus Deus* of Pius XII, to observe the action of the living magisterium of the Mystical Body of Christ relative to the definition of a dogma of faith, i.e., Our Lady's Assumption. Through such an analysis the student will come to see the prudential preparation made by the Supreme Pontiff in examining the sources for faith in the doctrine proposed for definition.

The competence of scholars in Sacred Scripture, theology, patristics, liturgy, as well as in the related profane sciences of archeology, history, linguistics, is brought to bear upon the search for proofs of Revelation communicated by Christ, as well as in the consistent belief and liturgical practice of the People of God through the centuries. But only when the doctrine is known with certitude to have existed in the deposit of Divine Revelation will it be considered definable.

Any of the following sources will give bibliographies important for this unit, as well as insights into the singular importance of the action of the Church in defining the Assumption of Our Lady as a dogma of the Church. Even a cursory reading on this subject will deepen the student's understanding of the exercise of the teaching authority of the Church and of the infallibility of the Supreme Pontiff in defining a dogma.

Cf. *American Ecclesiastical Review* for 1946, 1947, 1948, 1949, 1950.

Walter Burghardt, S.J. *The Testimony of the Patristic Age Concerning Mary's Death.* Westminster, Md.: Newman, 1957.

Juniper Carol. *Mariology,* Vols. I and II. Milwaukee: Bruce, 1955.

Marian Studies, Proceedings of the Mariological Society of America. Paterson, N. J.: 1950-1963.

Edward O'Connor, C.S.C. *The Mystery of the Woman.* Notre Dame: University of Notre Dame Press, 1956.

ADDITIONAL BIBLIOGRAPHY FOR COURSE

Barnabas M. Ahern, C.P. *New Horizons: Studies in Biblical Theology.* Notre Dame: Fides Publishers, 1963.

Georges Auzou. *The Formation of the Bible.* St. Louis: Herder, 1963.

Neal M. Flanagan. *Salvation History.* New York: Sheed and Ward, 1964.

Jacques Guillet. *Themes of the Bible.* Notre Dame: Fides Publishers, 1960.

Louis Hartman, C.SS.R., Trans. *Encyclopedic Dictionary of the Bible.* New York: McGraw Hill, 1963.

Roderick A. MacKenzie. *Faith and History in the Old Testament.* Minneapolis: University of Minnesota Press, 1963.

John L. McKenzie, ed. *The Bible in Current Catholic Thought.* New York: Herder and Herder, 1962.

————. *Myths and Realities: Studies in Biblical Theology.* Milwaukee: Bruce, 1963.
1963.

Celestine Luke Salm, F.S.C., ed. *Studies in Salvation History.* Englewood Cliffs, N. J.: Prentice-Hall, 1964.